Twenty Years of School-based Mass Shootings in the United States

Twenty Years of School-based Mass Shootings in the United States

Columbine to Santa Fe

Angelyn Spaulding Flowers
and Cotina Lane Pixley

LEXINGTON BOOKS
Lanham • Boulder • New York • London

Published by Lexington Books
An imprint of The Rowman & Littlefield Publishing Group, Inc.
4501 Forbes Boulevard, Suite 200, Lanham, Maryland 20706
www.rowman.com

6 Tinworth Street, London SE11 5AL, United Kingdom

British Library Cataloguing in Publication Information Available

Library of Congress Cataloging-in-Publication Data Available

Library of Congress Control Number: 2020944654

ISBN 978-1-7936-1313-4 (cloth)
ISBN 978-1-7936-1315-8 (pbk)
ISBN 978-1-7936-1314-1 (electronic)

This book is dedicated to those children, teachers, and school staff, who went to school one day and did not return.

Contents

Acknowledgments

This was a troubling subject on many different levels, but it was one that we felt required examination. We want to acknowledge and thank Dr. Sylvia I. B. Hill for her untiring assistance in reading revision after revision and for her insightful comments. We want to thank our families for their support and patience. Most importantly, we want to thank those teachers and school staff who try to make school a safe place for students to learn.

Introduction

In the United States, bullets flew in school buildings, athletic fields, school buses, or adjacent sidewalks ninety-six times in 2018. When the carnage ended, there were 59 people killed and another 109 injured. Three incidents that year accounted for almost 50% of the fatalities and 44% of the injuries. School shootings have increasingly intruded into the lives of families across the nation. As early as preschool, children are practicing what to do in the event there is an active shooter in their school. Parents confront the sobering reality that sending their children to school is akin to potentially sending them onto a firing range. While the public may falsely perceive this as an urban problem, the growing reality of school-based shootings in a variety of geographies has challenged this comfort zone for parents, school leadership, and the community as a whole.

The impetus for this book began after the mass shooting at Marjory Stoneman Douglas High School in Parkland, Florida, and was solidified three months later by the shooting at Santa Fe High School in Santa Fe, Texas. As mass shootings at schools continue, it has become increasingly clear that the mental illness causality attributed to these incidents is too narrow, and the continued reliance on that causal explanation impedes efforts to address the problem. The default position when a school-based mass shooting occurs is to immediately declare that the perpetrator must be mentally ill. This is understandable in that these acts are so horrendous that our minds recoil at the notion that a sane person could commit them. Psychological factors clearly are a key contributor. But this is not the same as suffering from a mental illness. Some of the perpetrators most likely did suffer from a serious mental disorder. The words "most likely" are used because very few of the perpetrators, for these school-based mass shootings, had a preexisting mental health diagnosis, and since many committed suicide at the end, they are not available for examination. Instead, law enforcement, the media, and the general public are left to make conclusions based on writings they left behind, social media posts, or perceptions by persons who knew them, which are at that point shaped by their last action. The problem is that continuing to use mental illness as the default explanation absolves society of the responsibility to seek other explanations for what is, at the most basic, a criminal act. It also absolves society of any reason to question its love affair with weaponry that, in many cases, arguably belongs on a battlefield.

School-based mass shootings are not a worldwide phenomenon. Absent a terrorist attack or act of war, mass shootings at schools are more likely to occur in the United States than in other nations. A school-based mass shooting is not limited to the confines of a specific location or individualized perpetrator motivation. It occurs within a larger environmental framework. We wanted to understand that environment. This book, therefore, approaches the examination of the twenty years of school-based mass shootings from Columbine to Santa Fe using a geospatial framework that examines incident variables within the context of the particular geographic space within which the incident occurred. The characteristics of the geographic space that were selected for examination include the impact of existing policy enactments such as federal and state gun laws, the role of a supportive gun culture, the relationship of socioeconomic demographics of jurisdictions and school communities, characteristics of the school-levels, types of weapons, and perpetrators.

These selected variables are by no means the only relevant characteristics. Nor are they covered in the fullest depth possible. Rather they provide identification and summary of issues that could lend themselves to subsequent more in-depth research. The intent is that consideration of these characteristics will provide an understanding sufficient to bring new impetus to the ongoing dialogue directed toward the crafting of effective public policy responses. To a large extent, the approach to this research can be compared to pulling threads from different places to see if they can be woven into an enhanced understanding of the phenomenon that is school-based mass shootings.

Columbine was selected as the starting point because school-based mass shootings changed in nature with the events that day at Columbine High School. On April 20, 1999, thirty-four students and staff were killed or injured by two students before they killed themselves. Columbine grabbed the attention of the nation. This was due in part to its high fatality count, but also due to the community within which it occurred. Columbine marked a turning point in the public's perception of the etiology of school-based mass shootings. Although not fully known or recognized at the time by the policymakers or academic scholars, this was not to be an isolated occurrence. Columbine was symptomatic of the beginning of a change in the landscape of school-based mass shootings. The twenty years that followed Columbine witnessed increasing carnage in school-based mass shootings. In that twenty years, an entire generation of young people had time to enter kindergarten and complete college. They have done this under the increasing shadow cast by the awareness that their school could be next.

To understand the reason for starting the examination with Columbine, a historical overview of school-based mass shootings is helpful. Columbine and its progeny are placed within a broader temporal perspective to demonstrate why the focus of the book is on the last twenty years of school-based mass shootings. It begins with an exploration of commonalities across all school-based mass shootings. For instance, a temporal analysis reveals the months when school-based mass shootings typically occur. This is the type of factor that could lend itself to inclusion in prevention strategies. Frequency of occurrence of school-based mass shootings, fatalities and injuries, as well as weapons, are compared for pre and post-Columbine school-based mass shootings. The primary distinction between pre-Columbine and post-Columbine school-based mass shootings is the higher number of fatalities for a smaller number of incidents. Three questions readily come to mind: Why these incidents occur? What can be done to prevent that occurrence? And most importantly, why post-Columbine is there a higher number of fatalities for a smaller number of incidents? These questions form the underpinning for this book. But it is understanding the third question that offers hope for the development of policy initiatives.

The environment within which these incidents occur forms the contextual framework for exploring these questions. The aspect which underlies, or overlies everything, is the law with its attendant policies, rules, and regulations. A hodgepodge collection of federal, state, and local laws comprise gun policy in the United States. Changing interpretations of the 2nd Amendment to the U.S. Constitution constitute the backbone of U.S. gun policy. The 2nd Amendment jurisprudence coupled with fifty years of federal firearms legislation provides a federal regulatory framework that now appears more directed toward the regulation of individuals than the regulation of firearms. Beyond federal requirements, which provide a minimum floor that each jurisdiction must meet, laws can vary from state to state. This enables individuals to acquire firearms in one state, which may not be legally acquired in an adjoining state and then illegally transport them back across state lines. This was not the case for school shooters. The weapons they used were legally available in their state of residence. This transitions us to consideration of the impact of location-based "gun culture" on school-based mass shootings. The laws in the states that have been the site of school-based mass shootings provide the underpinnings of a social and cultural milieu that can give rise to what has been identified as a "gun culture."

A "gun culture" is an environment that is supportive of guns. This research looks at the attributes of a "gun culture" and those attributes present in states that were the site of a school-based mass shooting. Leisure-time gun use, gun ownership, gun deaths (both homicides and suicides), and permissiveness of gun laws are aspects of gun culture that are explored for their impact. Mass shootings, in general, have been found to be related to both higher rates of gun ownership and permissive gun laws. This research explored whether this also holds true for the subset of mass shootings that occur at schools.

Once the extent of infusion of the gun culture in a region was determined, a new layer was added to the picture as the focus turned from regions and states to jurisdictions and communities. Bound up in the character of a particular geographic space, are the people who live in that space. A new level of complexity, socioeconomic factors were added. Demographic aspects such as population, income, education, families, housing, and households were explored for the jurisdictions, but particularly for the neighborhood surrounding the school. At one level, the idea was to get a sense of, or feel for, the neighborhood. This fed into a goal to determine if there were any distinctive characteristics of the communities surrounding schools that had been the site of school-based mass shootings. If so, could any of those characteristics be linked to characteristics of the mass shooting that had occurred at "their" school. This was further refined by analysis of the communities for the schools that suffered a high-fatality mass shooting, to identify similar and dissimilar community aspects.

At this point, we progressed down another notch to seek to understand the characteristics associated with the schools themselves. The most distinctive characteristic is the level of the school, whether it is an elementary, middle/junior high, or senior high school. Since Columbine, no mass shootings have occurred at stand-alone middle/junior high schools. This fact is not addressed in this research. What is explored is the different manner in which mass shootings occurred at elementary schools and high schools. The school levels were compared to themselves pre- and post-Columbine for identification of any changes that may have taken place over time. Post-Columbine, schools were compared across school levels, elementary schools to high schools. Key differences in perpetrators, and to a degree, weaponry were found. Mention of weapons is dispersed throughout the book. However, within the context of school levels, a more detailed discussion ensues that some may find unsettling in its detail.

This brings us to perpetrators, both as an aggregate unit and disaggregated. It is not possible to discuss school-based mass shootings without discussing the shooters, even if they are not the focal point. Sometimes it is believed that a perpetrator profile can be developed, and then it is simply a matter of watching for those who fit that profile. The reality is that there is no profile of a school-based mass shooter because the characteristics and traits that have been identified can be found in students who never end up as school shooters. The approach used in this book is to explore typologies that offer organizational classifications and models that offer an analytical framework.

In using the incident as the unit of analysis, it is recognized that the book does not incorporate the victims in its discussion. This is not because they are unimportant, but because there is nothing they could have done to avoid being victims. Our focus is on identifying factors that can be used to help shape policies that reduce or eliminate the creation of further victims. In that regard, the spirit of the victims permeates the book, even if they are not specifically examined. The one exception is that victim counts run throughout the book. This was intentional. It was meant to serve as a reminder that these "incidents" are not abstract discussion points, but rather that real people lost their lives. The inclusion of the shooter in the victim count (when they committed suicide) may be controversial. However, part of our purpose, to the extent possible, was to describe the level of the carnage to generate a sense of how the surviving school community was impacted. School-based mass shootings are unique among public mass shootings in that the shooter was typically part of that community and was known to either victims or survivors. Whether the post-shooting feelings generated are guilt or a sense of betrayal, they add to the trauma which the survivors suffer and the burden with which they must wrestle.

We are social scientists, so it is impossible for us to make a point without the incorporation of supporting data. As a result, the book is admittedly data-heavy in parts. Our purpose is to add to the needed conversations on school-based mass shootings through the identification of specifically desired public policy responses, as well as risk and protective factors. This will be facilitated by evaluating the convergence of variables from the range of school-based mass shootings. Our goal was not simply to identify problems, but to present a framework for the identification of solutions.

The question to be addressed is whether some common elements of these crimes can be analyzed to point to solutions. For instance, a school-based mass shooter is typically a white male, who is either a current or former student, and who often has some affinity for far-right extremist ideologies. The schools tend to be located in communities that are above the national median household income level, or at the least above the median household income for their surrounding jurisdiction. The weapons used were legally acquired, either by the perpetrator or by someone in their household. What do these factors mean when looking for solutions? Each chapter in this book was written to enable its use as a stand-alone chapter in this search for solutions. They were also written to provide a comprehensive conceptually layered examination when reading the book in its entirety.

Chapter 1

Historical Perspective on School-Based Mass Shootings

INTRODUCTION

School-based mass shootings neither began with Columbine nor ended with Santa Fe. The Center for Homeland Security and Defense reported a total of 1,340 school shootings from 1974 through the end of 2018.[1] The twenty-year period of 1999 to 2018 represents a snapshot in time, but it also represents the peak period to date. Based on trends, if everything stays the same, this period will itself be eclipsed. If, by fortuitous circumstance, this trend is reversed, the period will serve as an epoch whose underlying causes should still be studied, to avoid repetition. It is hoped that an examination of this particular snapshot will yield an understanding of school-based mass shootings that can be used to assist in crafting solutions. To understand the trajectory of school-based mass shootings from Columbine to Santa Fe, however, it is helpful to understand the historical context within which they reside.

When examining the hundred years from 1919 to 2018, the first school-based mass shooting does not appear until 1940. It left five dead and one injured. Since the shooter was a fired school employee, this first shooting in some respects can be also be considered a work-place violence incident. Foreshadowing future episodes at Red Lake, Minnesota (2005) and Newtown, Connecticut (2012), the shooting began elsewhere, subsequently traveling to the school.

On May 6, 1940, Verlin Spencer, a 38-year-old white male, walked into the administrative offices of the South Pasadena city school system for a hearing challenging his termination as principal of South Pasadena Junior High School.[2] Carrying a .22-caliber automatic pistol and 50 rounds of ammunition, he killed the superintendent, the principal of South Pasadena High School, and the District Business manager; and wounded the secretary of the

School Board. He then proceeded to the Junior High School where he stalked and killed two teachers.

Following a failed suicide attempt at the time of the incident and a subsequent guilty plea, Verlin Spencer eventually served thirty years in prison. This first school-based mass shooting contained elements found in future incidents as well as those that were less likely to occur. Twenty-one percent of shooters in subsequent school-based mass shooting incidents would also attempt suicide, some successfully and others unsuccessfully. Fewer served time in prison since they were killed by law enforcement personnel. This incident was an outlier in two respects. First, none of the victims were students. Second, while the typical school-based mass shooting is a planned event, despite pleading guilty, Verlin Spencer consistently claimed he did not remember these events. There is some support for this in that a blood test taken at the time of his arrest showed the presence of a chemical substance sufficient to render him legally insane.[3] It should be noted that failure to remember does not necessarily preclude planning.

The final school-based mass shooting covered by this book also occurred in May, although seventy-eight years later. In contrast to the 1940 incident with its five fatalities and one injury, the Santa Fe High School shooting left ten dead and thirteen injured. On May 18, 2018, Dimitrios Pagourtzis, a seventeen-year-old white male, walked into the arts complex at Santa Fe High School. Using a pump-action shotgun and a .38-caliber revolver, both of which were legally owned by his father, he began his shooting spree, which lasted for 32 minutes, resulting in the deaths of two teachers and eight students. These shootings were planned, and the individuals deliberately targeted. The shooter told police that he spared the lives of people that he liked so they could tell his story.[4] The Santa Fe shooting was the second worst school-based mass shooting in 2018. It is in the top five of all school-based mass shootings in terms of fatalities.

Following the shooting, it was alleged that Dimitrios Pagourtzis had been bullied by students and teachers, which the school denied (at least as to the teachers). He demonstrated extremist tendencies with an affinity for neo-Nazi artwork on his since-removed Facebook page.[5] His writings indicate that he was planning to commit suicide at the end. At the time this book was written, he had been found mentally incompetent to stand trial and sent to a mental facility for several months.[6] Dimitrios Pagourtzis potentially faces a sentence of life in prison with eligibility for parole after serving forty years.[7] In the seventy-eight years between the South Pasadena and the Santa Fe school-based mass shootings, there have been three notable changes over time: frequency of occurrence, number of fatalities and injuries, and type of weapons utilized. Following a discussion of the definition of the subject of this book, school-based mass shootings, these changes will be discussed.

DEFINITIONS

School-based mass shooting is a phrase that has, unfortunately, become ubiquitous. In this book, however, it has a specific meaning. The individual terms to be defined include school, school-based, and mass shooting. For the research described in this book, "school" refers to an educational institution serving students in grades K–12. The study excludes shootings at universities and colleges as well as day care centers. A shooting was considered "school-based" if it occurred within the confines of the school building, or if the shooting started within the school building and subsequently extended outside. Excluded were shootings that were gang-related, or shootings that occurred on the spur of the moment as a result of a fight. The focus of this book is on those incidents where the shooting was intentional and where the school environs were the main geographic target.

"Mass shooting" is a more challenging term. In the absence of a universally agreed-upon definition, it is difficult to get a commonly agreed-upon threshold number for a mass shooting. In the absence of a consistent definition, variance exists in the application. This is consistent with the findings of Booty et al. when they looked at four mass shooting databases and found that they included incidents that varied from database to database.[8] The Federal Bureau of Investigation (FBI) does not use the term "mass shooting." It uses the term "mass murder," which it defines as the killing of four or more people, not including the shooter, in one event, and at one geographic location.[9] Fox and Levin similarly define "mass murder" as the killing of four or more people within a single event. They noted that the event could range from a few minutes to several hours.[10] Following the December 2012 shooting at Sandy Hook Elementary School, Congress adopted the phrase "mass killing," defined as the killing of three or more individuals in a single incident.[11]

The subject of this research extends beyond mass murder or mass killings and focuses on mass shooting incidents. The book utilizes the definition adopted by the *Mass Shooting Tracker*,[12] which defines "mass shooting" as a single incident in which four or more people are shot. This definition includes those killed and injured and also includes the shooter. As used in this book, "mass shooting" provides a larger pool of school shootings for consideration than either "mass murder" or "mass killing." The inclusion of injuries, along with fatalities, paints a larger and more accurate picture of these incidents. Injuries are included because sometimes it is a single millimeter of difference in whether an individual ends up as a fatality, or it can be luck or modern medical advances. Those injured can suffer lifelong trauma or disabilities.[13] Injuries are such an integral part of the carnage that is a school-based mass shooting, that failure to count the injured does not appear to do justice to its victims. For the uninjured individuals in the school at the time of the shooting incident, the terror and subsequent mental trauma can be just as severe despite the lack of physical injury.

Inclusion of the shooter in the tally of injuries and fatalities is more debatable. The *Mass Shooting Tracker*'s inclusion of the shooter in their definition does differ from the typical manner in which mass shooting has been defined. Among seven databases, the *Mass Shooting Tracker* was the only one that included the shooter as part of the threshold fatality and injury count.[14] It should be noted that while six of those seven databases were titled "mass shootings," two of the six used a mass murder or mass killing definition, only counting fatalities to reach their threshold, thus excluding those injured.[15]

School-based mass shootings are a unique category of mass shootings that occur in a unique space. In most public mass shootings, witnesses or bystanders are less likely to know those who are killed or injured. In school-based mass shootings, on the other hand, the reverse is true. In a school-based mass shooting, victimization extends beyond the dead and injured. Also different from the typical public mass shooting is that in most school-based incidents, the perpetrator is known to other members of the school community. In school-based mass shootings, the overwhelming number of victims and perpetrators are juveniles. In these incidents, when the perpetrator dies, it is most frequently from a self-inflicted wound rather than from a law enforcement shooting. A comprehensive understanding of school-based mass shootings has to take this into account. For school-based mass shootings, failing to include the shooter in the threshold establishment decreases the available data for examination, thereby limiting the ability to understand this phenomenon.

This definition of school-based mass shooting was used to select the incidents incorporated into the database developed for this research. Three school shooting datasets incorporating a range of shootings and firearms presence on school campuses were reviewed. If combined, these datasets included thousands of incidents. Similar to the observation by Booty et al., there was variation in the shootings included in these three datasets. Using multiple databases for the initial culling served to broaden the potential incident pool. The incidents meeting the definitional criteria of this study were incorporated into a new consolidated dataset to be titled *U.S. School-Based Mass Shooting Database*.[16] The three school shooting databases utilized to elicit the data used to create a school-based mass shooting dataset were the source from which the mass shooting incidents were derived. These were the *K-12 School Shooting Database*, which extended back to 1970,[17] the *United States School Shootings and Firearm incidents 1990–Present*,[18] and *List of School Shootings in the United States*, which incorporated incidents as far back as the nineteenth century.[19] Unless otherwise indicated, all numerical and statistical data involving school-based mass shootings in this book are based on the consolidated *U.S. School-Based Mass Shooting Database*.

FREQUENCY OF OCCURRENCE

Frequency of occurrence examines when these incidents occurred, how often they occurred, and if there is an identifiable pattern to their occurrence. In taking a temporal look at school-based mass shootings, it was initially intended to look at the historical picture over the past hundred years. When attempting to identify the existence of a hundred-year pattern going back to January 1, 1919, the first noticeable fact was that it was necessary to leap forward twenty-one years to 1940 to find the first school-based mass shooting incident. It would be thirty-four years in 1974 before another incident occurred.

When viewed in the aggregate, the forty-four-year period from 1974 through 2018 averaged slightly less than one incident per year for a total of forty-two school-based mass shootings. In actuality, some years saw no incidents, while other years had multiple occurrences. In 1974, for example, there were two school-based mass shooting incidents, followed by one a year from 1975 through 1979. From 1974 through 2018, nine distinct periods encompassed a total of sixteen years, during which no school-based mass shootings occurred (see figure 1.1). It is important to remember that this does not mean that there were no school shootings during these periods. They either had fewer fatalities and injuries or did not meet some other aspect of the definition in use for this study.

Once the years with no incidents are excluded, twenty-eight years are left, during which forty-two school-based mass shootings occurred. When viewed from this perspective, the years during which school-based mass shootings occurred had an average of 1.5 incidents per year, ranging from one to three. As shown in figure 1.1, there were three school-based mass shootings in both 1997 and 2018. Ten years had two school-based mass shootings each. In 50% of those years, the shootings happened within a three-month period. A similar clustering also occurred in both of the years, which had three school-based mass shooting incidents. While there is insufficient data to assert the operation of a *copycat* phenomenon, it is argued that when one such incident occurs, schools need to be vigilant to avoid a repetition in their environs.

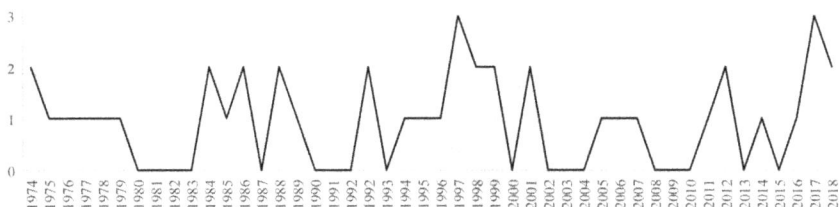

Figure 1.1   Number of School-Based Mass Shootings Annually 1974–2018. *Source:* Figure created by authors.

Towers et al. sought to evaluate the impact of media coverage of mass murders and school shootings on vulnerable individuals. They used a contagion model fitted against several school shootings and mass murder datasets to see if one such occurrence might increase the probability of a subsequent occurrence. Significant evidence of contagion was found.[20] Temporal patterns were identified in both school shootings and mass murders involving at least four fatalities.[21] Meindl et al. proposed a model of generalized imitation rather than contagion in examining the connection between media coverage of a first mass shooting event and the occurrence of a subsequent mass shooting event.[22]

School-based mass shootings took place across the entire school year. The only months not witnessing any incidents were the summer months of June through August. It is worth noting that many school districts are still in session during some part of June, others return to school in August, and some school districts have summer school. However, these are the months that appear to be free of school-based mass shootings. Everything being equal, it would be expected that the occurrence of school-based mass shootings is distributed fairly evenly across the school year. That does not turn out to be the case. The largest number of incidents occurred during the winter months (December, January, and February) when 42% of school-based mass shootings occurred. Thirty-two percent occurred in the spring months (March, April, and May). Twenty-six percent occurred in the fall (September, October, and November). It could be theorized that additional stressors occurring during the winter months contribute to the disproportionate level of school-based mass shootings at that time.

FATALITIES AND INJURIES

Five hundred forty-nine individuals have been either killed or injured in the forty-three school-based mass shootings identified in the past century for an average of eleven persons per incident. When it is considered that the most frequent number of persons victimized (those killed and injured) per incident is four, this average number is high. It indicates that there are some incidents where the number of victims pulls the overall average in an upward direction. Across all incidents, there is an aggregate fatality to injury ratio of approximately 1:3. The number of persons victimized per incident ranged from a low of four to a high of thirty-eight. This includes fatalities per incident ranging from zero to twenty-eight. Injuries went as high as seventy-four in a single incident from the explosion accompanying the hostage-taking at Cokeville Elementary School, which is described later in this chapter. Excluding that incident, injuries per incident ranged from one to thirty-two persons.

Table 1.1 School-Based Mass Shootings Exceeding Ten Combined Fatalities and Injuries

Date	School and Location	# Fatalities	# Injuries
Jan. 17, 1989	Stockton Schoolyard/Cleveland Elementary School Stockton, California	6	32
Apr 20, 1999	Columbine High School Littleton, Colorado	15	21
Mar. 21, 2005	Red Lake Senior High School Red Lake Minnesota	10	7
Oct. 2, 2006	West Nickel Mines School Nickel Mines, Pennsylvania	6	5
Dec. 14, 2012	Sandy Hook Elementary School Newtown, Connecticut	28	2
Feb. 14, 2018	Marjorie Stoneman Douglas High School Parkland, Florida	17	17
May 18, 2018	Santa Fe High School Santa Fe, Texas	10	13

Attention is understandably drawn to those shootings with ten or fifteen fatalities. It should be kept in mind, however, that approximately 84% of all school-based mass shootings resulted in five or fewer fatalities. Among those incidents with five or fewer fatalities, 20% had no fatalities at all. Since our definition of school-based mass shootings includes both deaths and injuries, a mass shooting with a low number of fatalities can still have injuries sufficient to bring it within the definitional standard of at least four persons killed or injured. Among the forty-three school-based mass shootings, the 16%, which had more than five fatalities, are listed in table 1.1. Of these seven incidents, each with more than five fatalities, only the shooting at Stockton Schoolyard/Cleveland Elementary School (1989) in Stockton California predated Columbine.

With thirty-two injuries and six fatalities, the Stockton Schoolyard/Cleveland Elementary School mass shooting was similar to many of the pre-Columbine incidents in that injuries outnumbered fatalities. However, it was the deadliest school shooting in the 1980s. The Stockton Schoolyard/Cleveland Elementary School mass shooting is also the first known school-based mass shooting involving the use of an AK-47 rifle. As is the norm with elementary school shootings, the perpetrator was an adult. In three minutes, Patrick Purdy, a 24-year-old white male, killed five children and wounded thirty-two others, including one teacher. Many of the children were Cambodian and Vietnamese immigrants. Patrick Purdy committed suicide before apprehension.

Unlike contemporary school-based mass shootings, which have led to outpourings of "thoughts and prayers," the Stockton Schoolyard/Cleveland

Elementary School shooting had a more practical impact. As a result of this incident, the State of California passed a law banning assault weapons (1989). Later that same year the administration of President George H. W. Bush banned the importation of assault weapons. Five years later, the Federal Assault Weapons Ban was passed (1994). In addition to prohibiting eighteen different types of assault weapons, the 1994 Federal Assault Weapons Ban also prohibited high-capacity magazine cartridges capable of holding more than ten bullets, as well as any firearms containing military-type features such as a bayonet mount, flash suppressor, or folding stock. At the time of its passage, already owned assault weapons were *grandfathered in*, allowing persons to keep those assault weapons which they already owned. The assault weapons ban included a ten-year sunset window expiring in 2004.

The past two decades have witnessed a substantial increase in school-based mass shootings. Forty percent (*n=43*) of the school-based mass shooting incidents in the past century have occurred in the last two decades. These two decades have seen both an increase in the number of incidents and an increase in the number of fatalities per incident. When looking at these fatalities over time, a trend is very apparent. Forty-two percent of the 549 victims of school-based mass shootings over the previous century were shot during the last two decades. Using Columbine as the locus, there were twenty-six school-based mass shootings pre-Columbine and sixteen after Columbine. Thirty-two percent of the injuries (*n=388*) but 65% (*n=161*) of the fatalities occurred in the twenty-year period that is the focus of this book.

As illustrated in table 1.2, Columbine and its progeny have had twice the number of fatalities despite accounting for less than one-half the number of incidents. The average number of fatalities per incident tripled when comparing Columbine et seq. to the pre-Columbine incidents. The twenty-six pre-Columbine school-based mass shooting incidents resulted in fifty-six fatalities. Post-Columbine, 17 school-based mass shootings resulted in 105 fatalities. Before Columbine, there was no school-based mass shooting incident with ten or more fatalities. Post-Columbine, almost one-third of school-based mass shooting incidents had ten or more fatalities. Pre-Columbine, the most frequently occurring number of fatalities in school-based mass shootings was one, with seven of the twenty-six incidents having only one fatality.

Table 1.2 Fatality and Incident Comparison: Pre- and Post-Columbine

	Number of Fatalities							Total # Fatalities	Total # Incidents	Average Fatalities per Incident
	0	*1*	*2*	*3*	*4*	*5*	*6*	*=>10*			
Pre-Columbine	4	7	5	5	2	2	1	0	56	26	2
Columbine to Santa Fe	3	2	3	2	0	1	1	5	105	17	6

When injuries are examined, the situation is reversed. Pre-Columbine, school-based mass shooting incidents were more likely to result in injuries than in deaths. The top 3 school-based mass shootings in terms of injuries, representing one-third of all 388 injuries in these 43 school-based mass shooting incidents, were pre-Columbine. Thurston High School (1998) in Springfield, Oregon, had twenty-four injuries and four fatalities. Stockton Schoolyard/Cleveland Elementary School (1989) in Stockton California, discussed previously, had thirty-two injuries and six fatalities. The largest number of injuries occurred at Cokeville Elementary School (1988) in Cokeville, Wyoming, with seventy-four injuries and two fatalities.

The incident at Cokeville Elementary School was noticeable for two reasons in addition to a large number of injuries. First, it was one of the three known hostage incidents in school-based mass shootings as well as the largest hostage-taking incident.[23] Second, the large number of injuries occurred not from the guns carried by the perpetrators, but from the gasoline bomb accidentally detonated by one of the perpetrators. On May 16, 1986, a husband and wife team Davis and Doris Young entered Cokeville Elementary School with an arsenal of weapons and a gasoline bomb.[24] Announcing they were leading a revolution, they confined 154 students, teachers, and staff in 2 classrooms. Davis Young attached the explosives to his wife and left the room. As Doris Young motioned to the hostages, the bomb accidentally detonated, she was engulfed in flames, and nearby children were burned. Upon returning to the room and seeing his wife on fire, Davis Young shot and killed her. He then shot the music teacher in the back of the head when he saw him attempting to escape through a window. The hostage crisis ended when Davis Young shot and killed himself. He and his wife were the only fatalities. Seventy-nine children were taken to hospitals in the region and treated for burns and smoke inhalation.[25]

Since all the injuries (excluding the music teacher and the perpetrators) resulted from the accidental explosion, it can be argued that Cokeville Elementary School should not be counted as a school-based mass shooting. It is included in this grouping, however, because it is consistent with other incidents where the perpetrators arrived with both guns and explosive devices. For instance, the Columbine shooting was initially intended to be a bombing. Eric Harris and Dylan Klebold placed two 20 pound propane bombs in the Columbine High School cafeteria. They resorted to shooting after the bombs failed to detonate.[26] At Cokeville Elementary School, while three people were shot, the only two fatalities were the two perpetrators, and the remaining injuries were from the explosion.

The Thurston High School mass shooting (1998) in Springfield, Oregon, with its twenty-five injuries and four fatalities, was the only school-based mass shooting among the top three injury count perpetrated by a juvenile.

Kip Kinkel, a fifteen-year-old white male, was upset at being suspended from school the day before and was facing possible expulsion. After killing both his parents, he walked into the Thurston High School cafeteria and began firing his father's Ruger .22-caliber rifle. At the time, he was also carrying 1,000 rounds of ammunition and 2 pistols.[27] Kip Kinkel killed two students and wounded twenty-five others. Failing in his suicide effort, he is currently serving a 110-year sentence in the Oregon Correctional System.[28] Similar to several of the incidents to be examined in the remainder of the book, Kip Kinkel killed his family members before going to school and launching his school-based mass shooting. Hidden behind the recitation of fatalities and injury numbers, in this case, is that Kip Kinkel is one of the few juvenile perpetrators treated for mental illness before the shooting.

WEAPONS

A handgun was used in one-half of all incidents overall where the type of weapon was known. The preferred handgun was the .22-caliber pistol. As illustrated in figure 1.2, since Columbine, 55% of the weapons used in

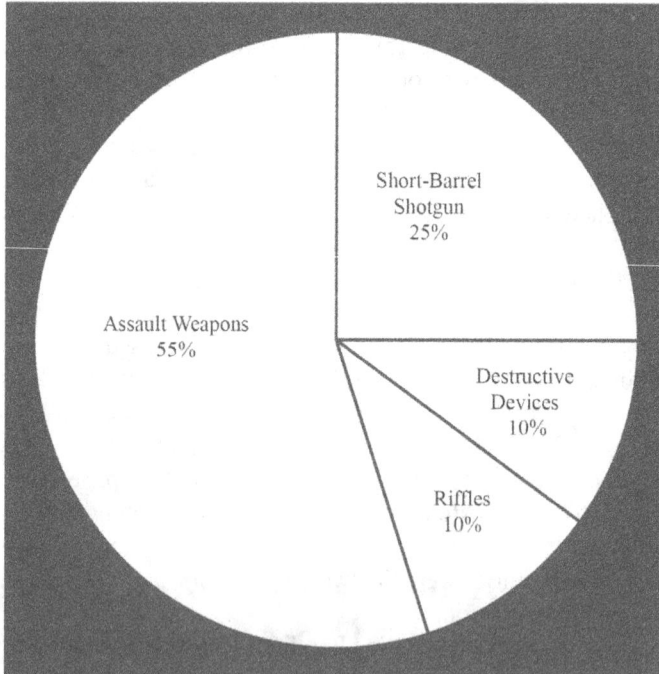

Figure 1.2   Weapons Used in School-Based Mass Shootings from Columbine Onward.
Source: Figure created by authors.

school-based mass shootings have been assault-type weapons (both automatic and semi-automatic). Short-barrel shotguns followed at 25%, then rifles at 10%. The remaining 10% were other destructive devices such as hand grenades, Molotov cocktails, and so on.

The only known use pre-Columbine of a semiautomatic type weapon was in the Stockton Schoolyard/Cleveland Elementary School Shooting (1989). Two years before Columbine, a rifle was used in the Pearl High School shooting (1997) in Pearl, Mississippi, by Luke Woodham, a sixteen-year-old white male. Before leaving home, he fatally stabbed his mother. Luke Woodham arrived at school with a rifle hidden under his trench coat. Once at school, he shot and killed two people, including his ex-girlfriend and wounded seven others.[29]

As the nature of the weapons changed with Columbine, so too did the relationship between fatalities and injuries in incidents. Pre-Columbine victims of school-based mass shootings were more likely to be injured. Since Columbine, victims are more likely to be killed. One inescapable question is whether there is a relationship between the increased lethality of available weapons and the increased number of fatalities. What is known is that regardless of the type of weapon used, the guns were all legally acquired. Since they were all legally acquired, the laws regarding weapons acquisition in the different jurisdictions become relevant.

Laws regarding weapons acquisition vary by state. Following the repeal of the federal assault weapons ban in 2004, states adopted a variety of restrictions on assault weapons. Some jurisdictions have outright bans on the purchase of assault weapons or high-capacity magazines. Other states, rather than regulating what can be acquired, regulate who is permitted to acquire weapons. In addition to mandatory universal background checks, the most common prohibitions typically exclude individuals from gun ownership who have: felony or violent misdemeanor convictions, a history of mental health, drug, or alcohol issues, or domestic violence convictions. Also in existence, but least likely, to be utilized are relinquishment laws and red flag laws. Relinquishment laws require that subsequently disqualified individuals turn in their guns. Red flag laws allow for the confiscation of guns from individuals whom a judicial proceeding has found to be a threat to themselves or others. Forty-eight states, and the District of Columbia, have at least one firearm restriction on the books. Two states, Montana and Idaho, have none. Even when present, the nature and extent of these laws vary by state.

CONCLUSION

A 100-year search, back to 1919, did not reveal a school-based mass shooting before 1940. Since that time, there have been forty-three incidents.

While Columbine and its progeny represent less than half of this total, they account for a disproportionate number of school shooting fatalities. Exploring post-Columbine shootings against the backdrop of the entire category of forty-three school-based mass shootings provides a more robust framework for highlighting and analyzing the changes that have occurred over the past twenty years. A look at incident frequency, fatalities, and injuries, as well as the weapons used in these school-based mass shooting incidents, highlights several themes lending themselves to further investigation in the shootings that are the subject of this book.

School-based mass shootings disproportionately occur during the winter months of December, January, and February. While not investigated in this book, this temporal anomaly presents intriguing areas for possible research. For instance, are there additional stressors in the winter months that might be contributing factors to the disproportionate levels of school-based shootings in the winter? Are those who perpetrate school-based mass shootings in the winter more likely to suffer from something like Seasonal Affective Disorder? What is happening in the school environment at this time that might be different from other times of the academic year? For example, was it the end of the academic quarter or semester at the schools where these shootings occurred, and could that be a possible factor? These are things that, at present, are not known.

What is known is that the number of school-based mass shootings has substantially increased in the past two decades. These two decades have also seen a disproportionate increase in the number of fatalities, with a corresponding decrease in the number of injuries. The decline in injuries is not because fewer people are getting shot, but because in this period they are more likely to be killed. One reason for the increased lethality of school-based mass shooting incidents since Columbine may be changes in the weapons used. Since Columbine, the majority of weapons used in school-based mass shootings have been assault-type weapons. Unlike many crimes involving guns, these weapons were legally acquired. While there are some federal laws governing guns, the majority are state-based, and as a result, it can vary from state to state. The upcoming chapter looks at the laws governing firearms at the national and state level and considers their role in the geospatial framework surrounding school-based mass shootings.

NOTES

1. See *K-12 SSDB Public* created by the Center for Homeland Defense and Security. https://www.chds.us/ssdb/.

2. (Rasmussen 1997).

3. Verlin Spencer was not informed of that information until three years later. At that time, bromide was the active ingredient in a very popular over-the-counter medication taken for headaches. It turned out to also be addictive. He took this medication several times daily for chronic headaches. Bromide was banned later that year (Rasmussen 1997).

4. (Frosh, Ailworth and Malas 2018).

5. (Turkewitz and Bidgood 2018).

6. (Lozano 2019).

7. (D'Angelo and Desk 2018).

8. (Booty et al. 2019).

9. (Federal Bureau of Investigation, Behavioral Analysis Unit, National Center for the Analysis of Violent Crime 2005).

10. (Fox and Levin 2003).

11. (Krouse and Richardson 2015).

12. (Mass Shooting Tracker 2018). The Mass Shooting Tracker is a crowd sourced database maintained by the Guns Are Cool subreddit.

13. (Booty et al. 2019).

14. (Everytown For Gun Safety 2019).

15. (Everytown For Gun Safety 2019).

16. (Lane and Flowers, U.S. School-Based Mass Shooting Database 2019).

17. (Center for Homeland Defense and Security n.d.).

18. (Ballotpedia n.d.).

19. (Wikipedia n.d.).

20. (Towers et al. 2015).

21. (Towers et al. 2015).

22. (Meindl and Ivy 2017).

23. The other two were: Lindhurst High School (1992, Olivehurst, California), and Frontier Middle School (1996, Moses Lake, Washington).

24. (Clark 2014).

25. (Clark 2014).

26. (History.com Editors 2009).

27. (Wilson 2018).

28. (Logan 2016).

29. (Zewe 1997).

Chapter 2

The U.S. Legal Framework for Firearms

INTRODUCTION

In the summer of 2019, three public mass shootings occurred during the same week. The first occurred on Monday, July 29, at the Gilroy Garlic Festival in California, one of the nation's best-known food festivals. Santino William Legan killed three persons and wounded twelve before killing himself. The AK-47 he used was legally purchased in the neighboring state of Nevada, but it could be neither sold nor transported in California where the shooting occurred.[1] Five days later, on Saturday, August 3, Patrick Crusius drove approximately 600 miles from outside Dallas, Texas to El Paso, Texas. At approximately 10:30 a.m. using an AK-47 style weapon, he killed twenty-two and injured twenty-seven in a Walmart. His pre-incident posted manifesto, and his post-incident statement to police, made clear that he deliberately drove to El Paso to kill Hispanics.[2] Fifteen hours later at 1:05 a.m. on Sunday, August 4, on the streets of downtown Dayton, Ohio, Connor Stephan Betts killed nine and injured twenty-seven as they were leaving clubs and restaurants on a weekend night. Betts was killed by the police 32 seconds after he fired his first shot. In those 32 seconds, Betts had hit thirty-six people. He was carrying an AR-15 style assault rifle and a 100-round drum magazine.[3] Two days later, it was reported by the media that after commenting that his daughter had been across the street from the shootings, an Ohio Congressman reversed his previous position and announced that he now backed a ban on military-grade assault weapons and high capacity magazines, and he supported strengthening "red flag" laws.[4]

Gun policy in the United States is an intertwined mosaic of federal, state, and in some cases, local laws. It is a constantly shifting area of jurisprudence. Each time a new mass shooting occurs, conflicting calls for strengthening or loosening gun regulations arise from elected officials. In what might be counterintuitive, a research study from the Harvard Business School found that following a mass shooting while there is no increase in enacted legislation to tighten gun restrictions, in Republican-dominated legislative bodies, legislation tends to be passed which makes it easier to own and use guns.[5] The legal landscape can change so quickly that the law may have changed between the time this chapter was written and the time the book was published. The issues relating to gun regulation are numerous enough to be the subject of their own book. Highlighting selected issues, this chapter is intended to provide a broad overview of the legal landscape in the United States relative to gun policy. It will paint the backdrop against which the school-based mass shootings discussed in this book occurred and can be viewed.

This chapter begins with a look at contemporary jurisprudence associated with the 2nd Amendment to the U.S. Constitution and a discussion of relevant federal firearms laws. Following this overview of the national gun framework, state utilization of selected prohibitions and regulatory requirements will be discussed.[6] This chapter will conclude with an examination of gun laws in the jurisdictions which have suffered school-based mass shootings in the twenty-year period from the mass shootings at Columbine High School in Littleton, Colorado, through the mass shootings at Santa Fe High School in Santa Fe, Texas.

FEDERAL FRAMEWORK FOR GUN REGISTRATION

The United States has a "federalist" system of government. This means that both the national government and the governments of the fifty states are each sovereign over those areas within their sphere of authority. The District of Columbia, as the nation's capital, is considered to be under Congressional authority.[7] In theory, this means that state laws govern everything within the subject matter and geographic boundaries of that state, whereas federal law governs the entire nation. But, since the highway system flows seamlessly from one state into the next, so too can the impact of one state's regulatory practices flow into adjoining states. As was evidenced by the public mass shooting at the Garlic Gilroy Festival in California, states with restrictive gun laws are menaced by an illicit interstate trafficking in firearms. A study of gun tracing data from the University of Pennsylvania School of Medicine found that 65% of the firearms recovered in restrictive states originate in adjoining states that have less restrictive firearm laws.[8]

The 2nd Amendment to the U.S. Constitution, which prescribes that "[a] well regulated Militia, being necessary to the security of a free State, the right of the people to keep and bear Arms, shall not be infringed"[9] is the beginning, and for some, the end of all discussion on firearms policy in the United States. The manner in which the U.S. Supreme Court has interpreted these twenty-seven words has had a profound impact on the type of regulatory schemes states are currently able to implement. For much of its existence, the 2nd Amendment was understood to be a prohibition against federal encroachment. States were free to adopt whatever regulatory scheme they chose. The death knell for that arguably constructionist approach was sounded in the 2008 case of *District of Columbia v. Heller*[10] and solidified two years later in *McDonald v. Chicago*.[11] Following an overview of judicial interpretation of the 2nd Amendment, this section will discuss the past fifty years of enacted federal legislation pertaining to firearms.

The Supreme Court and the 2nd Amendment

Prior to *Heller*, the definitive case was *U.S. v. Miller* (1939).[12] Jack Miller and Frank Layton were arrested and charged with transporting an unregistered firearm in interstate commerce from Oklahoma to Arkansas and failing to possess a stamp-affixed written order for that firearm as required by the relevant section of the National Firearms Act (NFA).[13] Miller and Layton were carrying a 12-gauge double-barreled Stevens shotgun. For purposes of this act, a firearm was defined as a shotgun or rifle having a barrel less than 18 inches in length or any other weapon that discharges a shot through the use of explosives and which can be concealed on a person. Also included in the definition of a firearm were machine guns, mufflers, and silencers, regardless of barrel length. Among the exclusions from this definition were pistols and revolvers, as well as rifles with a barrel length less than 18 inches, if the rifle was .22 caliber or smaller.

Miller and Layton argued that the NFA, rather than being a revenue-generating act (and thus permissible under Congressional power over taxation), was a usurpation of state powers and hence violated the 10th Amendment to the U.S. Constitution.[14] It was also alleged that the section in question of the Act violated the 2nd Amendment. The U.S. District Court for the Western District of Arkansas found that the NFA did violate the 2nd Amendment and accordingly quashed the indictment against Miller and Layton. The case was subsequently taken to the Supreme Court on appeal.

After a cursory dismissal of the 10th Amendment claim, the Supreme Court reversed the lower court and focused the bulk of its decision on an analysis of the 2nd Amendment issue. In reaching this decision, the Supreme Court construed the 2nd Amendment by treating the first phrase, "a well regulated militia...", as the condition precedent for the rest of the sentence. The court noted that "[i]n the absence of any evidence tending to show that possession or use of a 'shotgun having a barrel of less than eighteen inches in length' at this time has some reasonable relationship to the preservation or efficiency of a well regulated militia, we cannot say that the Second Amendment guarantees the right to keep and bear such an instrument."[15] The court in *Miller* placed extensive reliance on the laws regarding militias from the beginnings of the colonial settlements through the early years of the Republic. The court accepted as a given that the 2nd Amendment right, to keep and bear arms, was tied to the role of militias. This remained settled law for the next seventy years.

Unlike *Miller*, which rose to the Supreme Court as the result of a criminal conviction, *District of Columbia et al. v. Heller* (2008)[16] was a civil challenge to the District of Columbia's firearms law. The District of Columbia prohibited carrying an unregistered firearm. While other types of firearms, such as shotguns, could be registered, the law prohibited the registration of handguns. The District of Columbia statute permitted the Chief of Police to issue a one-year license for a handgun. Licensed handguns were required to be kept in an unusable state. They either had to be kept unloaded and disassembled, or they had to have a trigger lock. Richard Heller was a District of Columbia special police officer whose registration application to keep his handgun at home was denied. Heller sued arguing that those provisions of the law were in conflict with his 2nd Amendment right. In a 5–4 decision, the Supreme Court found in the 2nd Amendment an individual right to possess a firearm that was separate and distinct from militia service. The court found that this individual right included the right to use that gun for lawful purposes, including self-defense, inside the house. While finding that this right was not absolute, the court did find that it precluded the District's handgun ban and trigger-lock requirements since they had the effect of prohibiting an entire class of firearm overwhelmingly chosen by Americans for the purpose of self-defense.

In reaching its decision, the court treated the third sentence fragment of the 2nd Amendment "...the right of the people to keep and bear arms ..." as the operative and controlling fragment. The first two fragments, "a well regulated militia, being necessary to the security of a free State ..." appear to have been treated as subsidiary conditions. The rule propagated in *Heller* provides that the 2nd Amendment encompasses an individual right to keep and bear arms for the purpose of self-defense; states can regulate handguns, including registration and licensing systems, which include prohibitions against certain classes of individuals from owning handguns, but they cannot prohibit handguns. As *Heller* arose in the District of Columbia and concerned a District of Columbia statute, its result was to essentially limit the ability of the federal government to prohibit the keeping of handguns in the home for self-defense. What *Heller* did not do was clarify whether this prohibition also applied to the states. That matter was decided two years later in *McDonald et al. v. City of Chicago, Illinois et al.* (2010).[17]

The City of Chicago in 1982 became the first major city in the United States to enact a handgun freeze. Handguns purchased before the effective date of the law were permitted to be kept, but no new handguns could be purchased or registered. The lead plaintiff Otis McDonald, a 76-year-old retiree, owned several shotguns but felt a handgun would be more effective in his efforts to defend himself in his home. The Chicago ordinance in question allowed most residents to keep loaded shotguns and rifles. Following the decision in *Heller*, Mr. McDonald, along with others, filed suit challenging the constitutionality of Chicago's ordinance in light of the *Heller* decision. The Opinion of the Court in the *McDonald* case pronounced that the right of self-defense, which the *Heller* court found in the 2nd Amendment, was also applicable to the states, throwing out Chicago's handgun prohibition.

In January 2019, the U.S. Supreme Court agreed to take its first gun case in a decade for the term beginning in October 2019. The case of *New York State Rifle and Pistol Association et al. v. City of New York, NY* (2019) involved a challenge to a New York City ordinance limiting where individuals could transport their registered firearms.[18] The ordinance in question restricted the transportation of handguns to seven rifle ranges within the city limits but prohibited transportation outside of the city. In an effort to gain dismissal of the case by the Supreme Court, in July 2019, New York City amended its rules to permit registered handguns to be transported to second homes, businesses, and rifle ranges outside of the city. Notwithstanding this change, the Supreme Court heard oral arguments in this case on December 2, 2019. On April 27, 2020, the Supreme Court dismissed the case as moot in light of the changes New York City made to the rule.[19]

Federal Firearms Laws

Examination of enacted federal firearms legislation completes the underlying federal framework in regards to gun laws. Six laws will be discussed in this section. They are as follows: Gun Control Act of 1968 (GCA), Firearms Owners Protection Act of 1986, Brady Handgun Violence Prevention Act of 1993, Assault Weapons Ban of 1994, Protection of Lawful Commerce in Arms Act and Child Safety Lock Act of 2005, and the National Instant Background Check System Improvements Amendment Act of 2007. These statutes are a mix of regulatory restrictions and mandates. They also appear to be a mix of two distinct approaches to firearms violence. The GCA and the Assault Weapons Ban of 1994 target the firearms themselves in terms of restriction or regulation. The other four pieces of legislation target categories of individuals, limiting their ownership of firearms.

Gun Control Act of 1968

In the five years preceding passage of GCA, the nation witnessed the assassination of three national figures: President John F. Kennedy (November

1963), Reverend Dr. Martin Luther King, Jr. (April 1968), and Senator (and presidential candidate) Robert F. Kennedy (June 1968). The rifle that killed President Kennedy in 1963 was a mail order purchase from an advertisement in a magazine. It was five years, and two more high-profile assassinations before Congress passed legislation banning the mail-order sale of shotguns and rifles. The GCA was formally titled *An Act to amend title 18, United States Code, to provide for better control of the interstate traffic in firearms.*[20] In addition to regulating the interstate transfer of firearms, this act prohibited the importation of firearms with no sporting purpose. In a nod to U.S. companies, it did not restrict the domestic manufacture of these weapons. The GCA required that all firearms, whether domestic or imported, have an affixed serial number.[21] It imposed minimum age requirements for purchasing firearms and expanded the categories of individuals who were prohibited from possessing firearms. The act prohibited most felons, drug users, and individuals found to be mentally incompetent from purchasing a firearm.[22] This prohibition was intended to be accomplished at the point of purchase through the prospective purchaser answering "no" to the required questions. The GCA, however, did not impose a requirement that sellers verify the answers provided by the prospective purchaser.

If an individual is in the business of selling guns, the GCA requires a license and requires record-keeping. Collectors or others selling from their private collections that are not trying to make a profit are not required to get a Federal Firearm License. They do not have to keep records, and they do not have to perform background checks. These unlicensed dealers sell from their homes, online, and at gun shows. This has given rise to what has become known as the "gun show" loophole. An individual who would not be able to purchase a firearm from a federally licensed firearm dealer can acquire one from an unlicensed dealer at a gun show. The role of gun shows cannot be underestimated. A study by the Pew Research Foundation found that 25% of all gun owners say they go to gun shows often or sometimes.[23] While this category of sellers is not regulated by federal law, states have the option to impose regulations. As will be discussed later in this chapter, this is an option some states have chosen to exercise.

Firearms Owners' Protection Act of 1986

Almost twenty years after the passage of the GCA, the Firearms Owners' Protection Act of 1986 (FOPA) significantly revised many of the provisions of the GCA, thereby easing restrictions on firearms dealers.[24] This included limiting warrantless inspections of dealer premises by the Bureau of Alcohol, Tobacco, and Firearms (ATF); permitting sales by dealers at gun shows in the same state under their store license; eliminating the licensing requirement for ammunition sellers; and lifting the ban on the interstate transfer of ammunition to unlicensed buyers which then enabled the sale and shipping of ammunition through the U.S. Postal Service. The FOPA prohibited the establishment of a national or state registry system of firearm owners, firearms, or firearm transactions. It further prohibited the transfer of those records that are required by this act to a facility owned, managed, or controlled by a federal, state, or local jurisdiction.

Brady Handgun Violence Prevention Act of 1993

The Brady Handgun Violence Prevention Act of 1993[25] (The Brady Act) constituted another set of amendments to the GCA. These amendments were an effort to reduce gun violence by limiting access to guns through the imposition of a waiting period. The Brady Act imposed a five-day waiting period before a federally licensed dealer could complete the sale of a handgun to enable law enforcement to confirm that the buyer did not fall in a prohibited category. This addressed a weakness in the GCA, which relied on a purchaser's voluntary disclosure that they were in a prohibited category. The waiting period requirement of the Brady Act was not uniformly applicable. It excluded those who had either a federal firearm license or a state-issued permit such as a concealed carry permit since the state-issued permit required a state background check.

The five-day waiting period came with a five-year sunset provision. It was to be replaced with an *Instant Check* system known as the National Instant Criminal Background Check System (NICS), which would enable a seller to call a telephone number and find out instantly if a potential purchaser fell in a prohibited category.[26] The time could be extended to three days when necessary to clear the purchaser. If the results of the background check are not produced within those three days, then the purchaser is automatically cleared. The FBI found that in 2016 alone, there were 4,000 people who should have been denied, but were approved due to what has come to be called the "delayed denial" loophole.[27] During the previous year, Dylan Roof was one of the beneficiaries of this loophole. A white supremacist who wanted to start a race war, he walked into Emanuel A.M.E. Church in Charleston, S.C. on July 17, 2015, and killed nine African Americans while they were in a Bible study session.[28] Dylan Roof had a disqualifying felony drug conviction in the system. However, since his background check was not completed in the requisite three days, he was automatically cleared and was able to make his legal firearms purchase.

In addition to issues of timeliness, in order to be effective, NICS also requires a database that has accurate and complete information on individuals who are precluded for various reasons from purchasing a firearm. On April 16, 2007, Seung-Hui Cho killed thirty-two people on the campus of Virginia Tech in Blacksburg, Virginia, before killing himself.[29] Seung-Hui Cho was able to buy the weapons he used in what at the time was one of the deadliest mass shootings despite a judge's prior ruling that he was a danger to himself. Under the GCA, he should not have been able to purchase those weapons. However, the disqualifying information was never reported to NICS. To encourage states to report and update disqualifying information, the NICS Improvements Amendment Act of 2007 offered financial incentives.[30] The goal was to prevent disqualified persons from being about to legally purchase a firearm.

The 2017 shooting at the First Baptist Church in Sutherland, Texas, is illustrative of the continuing shortcomings in this system. On Sunday, November 5, 2017, Devin Patrick Kelley entered the First Baptist Church in Sutherland, Texas, armed with a Ruger AR-566 (semiautomatic rifle) and a handgun.[31] In the end, there were twenty-six people dead and another twenty injured. Devin Patrick Kelley had a domestic violence conviction that was never entered into the required database by the U.S. Air Force. As with Seung-Hui Cho, if the information had been available to NICS, the routine check would have flagged Devin Patrick Kelley as an ineligible purchaser. A decade after the passage of the NICS Improvement Act, disqualifying information is still not making it into the system.

Public Safety and Recreational Firearms Protection Act of 1994

The Public Safety and Recreational Firearms Protection Act, or the Assault Weapons Ban of 1994 (AWB) as it is more commonly known, was part of the Violent Crime Control and Law Enforcement Act of 1994.[32] It prohibited the domestic manufacture[33] for civilian use of certain types of semiautomatic firearms and large-capacity ammunition magazines. Prohibited weapons were either specifically listed,[34] or met a two-prong test,[35] for example, a semiautomatic shotgun with two or more of the following: folding or telescoping stock, pistol grip, or detachable magazine. There were similar-type definitions for semiautomatic assault rifles and pistols. The AWB did not prohibit all assault weapons. Otherwise prohibited weapons that were legally acquired and were manufactured before the date of this legislation were *grandfathered in*, and were still able to be possessed and transferred legally.[36] The law included a sunset provision whereby the ban on assault weapons would automatically expire after ten years. During the ten years that this law was in effect, total mass shootings as well as total victims, injuries, and fatalities were lower than the ten years immediately preceding and the ten years immediately following.[37]

*Protection of Lawful Commerce in Arms Act
and Child Safety Lock Act of 2005*

The purpose of the 2005 Protection of Lawful Commerce in Arms Act (PLCCA) is most clearly described by its long title *An Act to prohibit civil liability actions from being brought or continued against manufacturers, distributors, dealers, or importers of firearms or ammunition for damages, injunctive or other relief resulting from the misuse of their products by others.*[38]

Prompted in large part by lawsuits brought against firearms manufacturers by victims of gun violence and by local jurisdictions, this act granted widespread immunity to manufacturers and sellers of firearms and ammunition when their product was misused or criminally used.[39] The PLCCA addressed the concern that lawsuits against gun manufacturers could eradicate the domestic gun manufacturing industry. Also included in this legislation was the Child Safety Lock Act of 2005[40] (CSLA), which required (with a few exceptions) that all guns sold or transferred had to be equipped with a safety device or secure storage. Once the gun was made inoperable through storage or a locking device, the CSLA operated to immunize gun owners from civil liability in situations where their handgun was unlawfully used by a third party. The combined effect of the PLCCA and the CSLA was to create a protective bubble around an arguably dangerous product that nonetheless shielded anyone legally associated with it from liability when that product produced harmful results.

Efforts have made efforts to pierce that bubble. On December 14, 2012, after killing his mother, Adam Lanza walked into Sandy Hook Elementary School and fired 156 shots killing 20 children and 6 adults in five minutes.[41] In 2015, a surviving teacher and the families of nine victims filed suit in Connecticut State Courts arguing among other issues that the marketing strategies of Remington Arms and its subsidiary Bushmaker violated Connecticut's statute on deceptive marketing.[42] The trial court denied this allegation. However, the Connecticut Supreme Court remanded the case back to the lower court, finding that the plaintiffs should have been given the opportunity to prove that Remington had violated the Connecticut Unfair Trade Practices Act (CUTPA). In making the remand, the Connecticut Supreme Court did not rule that the Connecticut statute had, in fact, been violated. Instead, they determined that the Sandy Hook families should have been given the opportunity to present evidence on that issue at the trial court level. Arguing that this suit is precluded by the PLCCA and that the remand was therefore improper, in August 2019, Remington Arms asked the Supreme Court to hear this case in its upcoming term.[43] The Supreme Court denied the Remington Arms appeal on November 12, 2019.[44] This permits the case to go back to the trial court for a determination of whether Remington Arms had violated CUTPA.

THE STATE FRAMEWORK

The federal laws regulating firearm sales only apply to federally licensed firearms dealers, that is, those sellers who are in the business of selling firearms. They do not apply to the large number of sales by private individuals or collectors, or those individuals who sell firearms but for whom it is not a business. Miller et al. in a self-report survey of gun owners found that 50% indicated that in the previous two years, they acquired weapons without a background check when engaged in a private gun sale.[45] Nor do the federal laws apply to transfers of firearms among individuals that are not sales. Since the expiration of AWB, state regulations are the only existing regulations governing assault weapons. Within the parameters of the 2nd Amendment, states can add requirements to existing federal laws, but they cannot negate them. Following a brief summary, three categories of regulation will be discussed: age restrictions, background check requirements, and assault weapons bans. Age restrictions are of particular importance when examining school-based mass shootings where the majority of perpetrators are students.

Forty-eight states and the District of Columbia have adopted at least one firearm restriction. Two states, Montana and Idaho, have none. Of the state firearm restrictions to be discussed, the largest number of states, 31% have only one restriction. When reviewing the gun-related laws in the fifty states and the District of Columbia, the most common prohibitions are prohibitions for high-risk individuals and prohibitions for individuals with domestic violence convictions. High-risk individuals are those persons who have been convicted of a felony or a violent misdemeanor; individuals with a history of mental health, drug, or alcohol issues; or those a court considers to be dangerous. Forty-five out of fifty-one jurisdictions have prohibitions in this area.[46] Thirty-four out of fifty-one jurisdictions prohibit the sale of firearms to persons with domestic violence convictions. In some jurisdictions, the prohibitions on persons with domestic violence convictions also include individuals with domestic violence related restraining orders or with convictions for stalking. Another popular area for state regulation is background checks.

Among the type of restrictions least likely to be reflected among state statutes are relinquishment laws and red flag laws. Federal laws prohibit certain categories of individuals from purchasing firearms. But what happens if an event, that would have disqualified an individual from purchasing a firearm if it had occurred before the purchase, does not occur until after the purchase? Absent some other restriction, the individual would get to keep their weapons. A small number of states have stepped into this vacuum. Seven jurisdictions specify that those individuals who have subsequently become disqualified from possessing a firearm are required to turn them in, to law enforcement. Five jurisdictions allow law enforcement personnel to initiate a process to confiscate firearms from individuals whom a judicial proceeding has found to be a threat to themselves or others. Red flag laws permit the police or a family member to petition a state court to temporarily remove the guns from an individual suspected of being a danger to themselves or others.

An affirmative right to the use of firearms is reflected in a category of laws known as *stand your ground* laws, which are on the books of twenty-six states.[47] These laws expand the right to use deadly force when threatened beyond the home environs, to any place where the individual has a right to be, typically, on public space. While not the subject of this research, it should be noted that *stand your ground* laws have become notorious in the shooting deaths of unarmed young men of color, on public space, by white men. *Stand your ground* laws typically appear in places with two or fewer firearm restrictions or prohibitions on their books.

Age Restrictions

In their study of the impact of minimum age requirements for purchase or possession of firearms, the Rand Corporation noted that states approach minimum age requirements in one of two ways, either a prohibition on the sale or transfer of weapons or a prohibition on possession.[48] Eleven states and the District of Columbia prohibit purchasing or selling a handgun through a private dealer[49] if the purchaser is under the age of twenty-one.[50] These states are Massachusetts, Rhode Island, Connecticut, New York, New Jersey, Ohio, Maryland, Delaware, Iowa, Illinois, Hawaii, and the District of Columbia. With the exception of Ohio, Rhode Island, and Delaware, these states also prohibit possession of a handgun if you are under the age of twenty-one. Since federal law places no minimum age requirement in regards to the possession of long guns,[51] states are free to develop their own laws. Several states have done so. Fourteen states have prohibitions against long gun purchases to individuals under the age of eighteen. Illinois and the District of Columbia require that individuals be at least twenty-one to purchase a long gun.[52] Some states expressly permit the purchase of a firearm at a younger age. Montana allows the purchase of a long gun at the age of fourteen.[53] Alaska, Maine, Minnesota, New York, and Vermont require that an individual be sixteen to purchase a long gun, while Vermont also permits the purchase of a handgun at sixteen.[54]

State Required Background Checks

Twenty-one states and the District of Columbia require some type of background check.[55] These background checks are intended to identify those persons who are ineligible to purchase firearms based on the types of disqualifying factors discussed above for high-risk individuals. There are five different approaches to background checks currently utilized by these states. Eleven states and the District of Columbia require universal background checks for all firearms purchases. Two states require background checks at the point of sale for handguns, but not long guns. Three states require that a permit be obtained by all firearms purchasers; the permit is issued after a background check. A permit and background check system is used by four states, requiring a permit and a background check for handguns but not long guns. One state requires a permit to purchase a firearm, and if the sale is from an unlicensed seller, then the unlicensed seller must conduct the sale through a federally licensed firearms dealer (who is required by federal law to conduct a background check). In the twenty-nine states that do not have a state background check requirement, the only existing background check requirement is the federal one, which only applies to those purchasing from federally licensed firearms dealers.

State Bans of Assault Weapons and High-Capacity Magazines

In the twenty-year period between Columbine and Santa Fe, assault weapons emerged as a primary weapon of choice. Presently one out of five jurisdictions nationwide ban or regulate assault weapons. One out of six jurisdictions ban high-capacity magazines.[56] It is the ban on high-capacity magazines that some experts believe may hold the most promise in reducing the number of victims when these incidents do occur.[57] In a study of public mass shootings between 1983 and 2013, Lemieux found that it was firepower capacity rather than the type of weapon that was more closely associated with the number of fatalities.[58] In other words, the more ammunition that could be discharged without having to stop and reload, the more individuals who would be hit.

Following the 2012 school-based mass shooting at Sandy Hook Elementary School, the states of Colorado, Maryland, New York, as well as Connecticut passed major gun control legislation.[59] Connecticut, the site of the Sandy Hook school shooting, passed the nation's strictest gun control law. This law banned: gun magazines with a capacity of more than ten rounds; required background checks for private gun sales, even those occurring at gun shows; and expanded the state's assault weapons ban to include an additional 100 gun models.[60] Nine states, as well as the District of Columbia, also ban high-capacity magazines.

GUN LAWS IN STATES WITH SCHOOL-BASED MASS SHOOTINGS

There have been seventeen school-based mass shootings from the April 20, 1999, incident at Columbine High School in Littleton, Colorado, through the May 18, 2019, incident in Santa Fe, Texas. These seventeen incidents have occurred in twelve different states.[61] California, Ohio, and Washington have had multiple school-based mass shooting incidents during this period. The remainder of this chapter will examine the issue of whether there are identifiable differences in the types of gun laws previously discussed, between states which have been the site of school-based mass shootings and those which have not.

Among the states which have been the site of school-based mass shootings since Columbine, 25% presently ban assault weapons. These states are California, Connecticut, Minnesota, and Washington State. The first assault weapons ban in the nation was passed in California in 1989 following the 1989 school-based mass shooting at Stockton Schoolyard/Cleveland Elementary School, which killed five children and one teacher while wounding another thirty-two individuals. This was the first known use of an assault weapon in a school-based mass shooting. The weapon used was an AK-47. California has had three school-based mass shootings since the adoption of that ban. It should be noted that it took the fatalities from all three of the post-Columbine California incidents to equal the fatality count in the Stockton Schoolyard/Cleveland Elementary School mass shooting.

The five deadliest school-based mass shootings have occurred in Colorado, Minnesota, Connecticut, Florida, and Texas. Among these states, Connecticut and Minnesota had assault weapons bans that predated the shootings. However, in both of these states, the weapons used in the school-based mass shooting were still legally acquired. In short, despite the presence of a ban on assault weapons, it was still possible in those states for individuals to legally possess an assault weapon. Eighteen percent ($n=38$) of the states which have not been the site of a school-based mass shooting during this period, presently have an assault weapons ban.

Connecticut tightened their assault weapons ban following the mass shooting at Sandy Hook Elementary School. In Connecticut, Adam Lanza killed twenty children and six adults with a Bushmaster Model XM15-E2S rifle.[62] A Bushmaster .223-caliber rifle and two handguns were found next to his body after he was killed by law enforcement, and an Izhmash Saiga-12, 12-gauge semiautomatic shotgun was in his car.[63] All of these weapons were purchased by Lanza's mother as a straw purchaser for Lanza. She was the first person he killed that day. Jeffery Weise killed ten people, including himself, on the Red Lake Indian Reservation in Minnesota. Following a similar pattern to

Adam Lanza, he used his grandfather's Glock pistol and shotgun to first kill his grandfather and his grandfather's girlfriend. Jeffery Weise then went to school, where he killed a school security guard, a teacher, and five students before killing himself.[64] These weapons were legally used by Weise's grandfather in his role as a Tribal police officer.[65]

Half of the twelve states that have been the site of school-based mass shootings since Columbine have some type of background check requirements. Among those states which have been the site of a school-based mass shooting, California, Colorado, Connecticut, and Washington have a universal background check requirement at the point of sale for handguns and long guns (such as rifles or shotguns).[66] The permitting and background check systems in Pennsylvania and Nebraska focus only on handguns with no comparable requirements for long guns. Pennsylvania requires a background check at the point of sale for handguns while Nebraska has a permit and background check requirement for handguns.[67] Florida, Georgia, Kentucky, Minnesota, Ohio, and Texas do not have a state background check requirement.[68] Forty-three percent of the states ($n=38$), which have not been the site of a school-based mass shooting, have some type of background check requirement.

In distinguishing states which have been the site of a school-based mass shooting from those which have not, the most relevant restriction may be "the age restriction." Sixty-five percent ($n=8$) of the states which have been the site of a school-based mass shooting and do not have an assault weapons ban also do not have a minimum age for possession of long guns.

In comparison, 50% ($n=32$) of the states which have not had a school-based mass shooting and lack an assault weapons ban also do not have a minimum age for possession of long guns. This is equivalent to a 25% differential between these states that were and those that were not the site of a school-based mass shooting in the post-Columbine era. Since there is no federal minimum age for long gun possession, this means that in the absence of a state minimum, none exists. The arguable purpose for the absence of a minimum age for long gun possession is that these are the types of guns with which juveniles and adults engage in recreational activities such as hunting.[69] But, the impact is that young people in these states have access to and familiarity with the use of guns at an earlier age than in states which do have a minimum age for possession.

CONCLUSION

The legal landscape in regards to firearm regulation is mixed. To a large extent, the federal government appears to have abandoned efforts to regulate firearms. It can be argued that the existing federal framework on firearms regulation is largely directed more toward regulating classes of individuals than regulating firearms. When coupled with the *Heller* and *McDonald* decisions from the U.S. Supreme Court, for the past decade, states and localities have also seen their regulatory ability restricted.

Those areas which remain a permissible subject of state regulation are often rendered ineffective through individual or institutional reporting failures. More importantly, these efforts are undermined by the practical invalidation of restrictive laws in one jurisdiction by porous state borders, which allow the trafficking of firearms across state lines from permissive jurisdictions. At the state level, this chapter looked specifically at background checks, assault weapons bans, and age restrictions comparing those states which were and were not the site of school-based mass shootings. It was found that states which were the site of school-based mass shootings were more likely to be states which lacked both an assault weapons ban and a minimum age requirement for possession of a long gun.

The newest entry into gun regulation has been the corporate sector. Some national chains have started to either expressly disallow or request that customers not carry weapons on their premises. A partial listing of these companies includes Panera Bread, Chuck E. Cheese, AMC Theatres, Regal Entertainment Group, Starbucks, Target, Costco, Chipotles, and Giant Food.[70] Walmart is the latest addition. The seller of a large number of firearms, Walmart announced it will no longer sell ammunition and is requesting that people not carry firearms in the store. This announcement was made less than a month after the mass shooting and targeting of Hispanics in the Walmart in El Paso Texas

The legal and regulatory framework for firearms policy is only one part of the total environment within which school-based mass shootings occur. The next chapter will add a cultural dimension to the examination of firearms policy at the state and regional level.

NOTES

1. (Simon, Leveson and Simon 2019).
2. (Danner 2019).
3. (de la Garza and Zenee 2019).
4. (Baker 2019).
5. (Luca, Malhotra and Poliquin 2019).
6. In this context, "state" refers to the fifty states and the District of Columbia.
7. Congress is delegated the power to "exercise exclusive Legislation in all Cases whatsoever, over such District (not exceeding ten Miles square) as may, by Cession of particular States, and the Acceptance of Congress, become the Seat of the Government of the United States" U.S. Constitution, Art. 1, § 8 (17). The District of

Columbia Home Rule Act Pub.L.93-198 provides a limited measure of self-govern-
ment for the residents of the District of Columbia.

Congress however, has reserved to itself ultimate controlling power. This
includes for example: the power to approve the spending of funds; approve and dis-
approve any laws passed by the elected Council of the District of Columbia; make
its own laws governing daily life and operations of the city and its local government
functions, and so on. It has been suggested that in this instance Congress is merely
exercising the same relationship of a state to one of its localities. The difference however is that unlike a state legislature vis-à-vis the resident of that state, residents of
the District of Columbia do not have voting representation in the U.S. Congress, even
though those residents pay more per capita in federal income taxes than residents of
the fifty states. See (Associated Press 2017).

8. (Hoofnagle et al. 2019).

9. (United States Consitution, Amendment 2 1789).

10. (District of Columbia v. Heller 2008).

11. (McDonald et al. v City of Chicago, Illinois et al. 2010).

12. *United States v. Miller* et al. (1939) 307 U.S. 175.

13. Act of June 26, 1934. 48 Stat. 1236-1240, 26 U. S. C.§ 1132.

14. *"The powers not delegated to the United States by the Constitution, nor prohibited by it to the States, are reserved to the States respectively, or to the people."*
U.S. Constitution, Amendment 10.

15. (United States v Miller et al. 1939), pg. 178.

16. (District of Columbia et al. v. Heller 2008).

17. (McDonald et al. v City of Chicago, Illinois et al. 2010).

18. (New York State Rifle and Pistol Association et al. v. City of New York, NY
2019).

19. (New York State Rifle and Pistol Association et al. v. City of New York, NY
2020).

20. (Gun Control Act 1968).

21. (Gun Control Act 1968) amending 26 U.S.C. §5842(a).

22. (Gun Control Act 1968) amending 18 U.S.C. Chapter 44 §922(d).

23. (Parker et al. 2017).

24. (The Firearms Owners' Protection Act 1986).

25. (The Brady Handgun Violence Prevention Act 1993). This legislation was
named after James Brady, former press secretary for President Ronald Reagan. James
Brady was seriously injured and permanently disabled in the 1981 assassination
attempt on President Reagan. James Brady and his wife Sarah subsequently devoted
their lives to gun control efforts. James Brady died in 2014 as a result of the wounds
sustained in 1981.

26. (The Brady Handgun Violence Prevention Act 1993 §103(b)).

27. (Voght 2019).

28. (Sanchez and Payne 2016).

29. (CNN Library 2019). The mass shooting at Virginia Tech is not included in
this study since it was not a K–12 school. However it does present an example of a
weakness with the background check system.

30. (NICS Improvement Act 2007).

31. (Hanna and Yan 2017).

32. (The Violent Crime Control and Law Enforcement Act 1994).

33. An Executive Order prohibiting the importation of foreign made semi-automatic weapons lacking a sporting purpose was issued by President George H. W. Bush following the shooting at the Stockton Schoolyard Cleveland Elementary School in Stockton California on January 17, 1989 where six people were killed and thirty-two injured.

34. (The Violent Crime Control and Law Enforcement Act 1994), Title 11, §110106 Appendix A, Amending 18 U.S.C. §922.

35. (The Violent Crime Control and Law Enforcement Act 1994), Title 11, §110101(b).

36. (The Violent Crime Control and Law Enforcement Act 1994), Title 11 §110102(a)(2).

37. (Lemieux 2014).

38. (Protection of Lawful Commerce in Arms Act 2005).

39. 18 U.S.C. §7902.

40. (Protection of Lawful Commerce in Arms Act 2005) §5.

41. (Lupica 2013).

42. (Altimari 2019).

43. (de Vogue and Jorgenson 2019).

44. (Chan 2019).

45. (Miller, Hepburn and Azrael 2017).

46. (Giffords Law Center to Prevent Gun Violence (a) n.d.).

47. (Lemieux 2014).

48. (RAND 2018).

49. Sales by persons in the business of selling firearms are covered by federal law.

50. (RAND 2018).

51. A long gun has a longer barrel, usually requires two hands, and is supported by the shoulder when fired. The National Firearms Act of 1934 defined a riffle has having a barrel length of at least 16 inches and a shotgun as having a barrel length of at least 18 inches.

52. (RAND 2018).

53. (RAND 2018).

54. (RAND 2018).

55. (Giffords Law Center to Prevent Gun Violence (b) n.d.).

56. (Giffords Law Center to Prevent Gun Violence 2018).

57. Interview of David Chipman of the Gifford Center who has twenty-five years' experience as a special agent with Bureau of Alcohol, Tobacco, and Firearms (ATF) conducted by William Brangham (Public Broadcasting Service 2019).

58. (Lemieux 2014).

59. (Wilkie 2013).

60. (Wilkie 2013).

61. (Lane and Flowers 2019).

62. (CNN Library 2019).
63. (CNN Library 2019).
64. (Enger 2015).
65. (Enger 2015).
66. (Giffords Law Center (b) n.d.).
67. (Giffords Law Center (b) n.d.).
68. (Giffords Law Center (b) n.d.).
69. (RAND 2018).
70. (Duva 2014).

Chapter 3

Guns, Culture, and School-Based Mass Shootings

The Regional and State Context

INTRODUCTION

States that were the site of a school-based mass shooting during the twenty years stretching from the 1999 shooting at Columbine High School in Littleton, Connecticut, through the 2018 shooting at Santa Fe High School in Santa Fe, Texas, are examined in this chapter. Research has been fairly consistent over time in finding associations between variations among jurisdictions in their relationship to guns and the levels of gun violence in those jurisdictions. Two of the most frequently heard but competing explanations for gun violence and mass shootings—culture and lax gun laws—were examined in a multilevel quantitative study by Lemieux.[1] Of particular relevance for this chapter was the meso-level comparison of the fifty states and the microlevel comparison of seventy-three public mass shootings in the United States.[2] Among the findings were that the Southern gun violence culture was a predictor for and associated with the firearm murder rate and that a reduced firearm capacity is associated with reduced victims. This is consistent with Felson et al. who noted that regional differences in gun violence had been found to be reflective of a gun culture among southern and western whites.[3]

Vizzard noted that homicide is typically a spontaneous action enabled by the availability of firearms and that these spontaneous actions are culturally and geographically concentrated.[4] Towers et al. found a significant association between the state prevalence of firearms and the state incidence of mass killings with firearms, school shootings, and mass shootings.[5] An examination of gun owners from 1998 to 2015 found that states with more permissive gun laws and higher rates of gun ownership tended to have more mass shootings than states with more restrictive gun laws.[6] These studies looked at mass shootings in general and were not limited solely to school-based mass shootings. Although school-based mass shootings can be considered as a subset of mass shootings, there are notable differences that may preclude the general applicability of these findings. As will be discussed below, studies have found associations between the availability of guns and suicides in particular jurisdictions.[7] Other studies have found an association in the availability of guns and homicides in a jurisdiction.[8] The question arising is the extent to which these findings also extend to school-based mass shootings.

The issue explored in this chapter is the extent to which a regional gun culture also embraces the school-based mass shootings that occur in that region. Another way to consider this issue is the extent to which there are identifiable and distinct regional characteristics of school-based mass shootings, and whether those characteristics conform to the expectations associated with the region's gun culture or lack thereof. This chapter begins with an examination of a demographic analysis of U.S. regions and associated gun use (both legitimate and illegitimate) before delving down into the specific states that have been the site of school-based mass shootings in the past twenty years. It takes a snapshot-in-time look at regional and state differences in regard to gun culture. A more detailed microlevel community analysis of the local geographic space where these incidents occurred when they occurred will take place in a subsequent chapter.

REGIONAL GUN CULTURE ANALYSIS

By 2018 it was estimated that 327,167,434 individuals lived in the United States.[9] The U.S. Census Bureau divides the country into four regions, which are further subdivided into nine divisions. Approximately 38% of the population lives in the South, which includes sixteen states and the District of Columbia.[10] This was followed by the West with thirteen states and 24% of the nation's population, the Midwest with twelve states and 21% of the nation's population, and the Northeast with nine states and 17% of the nation's population.[11] These percentages have remained relatively unchanged over the previous decade.

This section will compare the regions relative to their respective gun cultures. While a gun culture can be reflected by the willingness to carry weapons in public for self-defense or otherwise (as was studied by Felson et al.), a gun culture can also be identified by the role of guns in leisure-time activities. In addition to the extent of leisure time gun use, this section will examine gun ownership patterns, gun deaths, and the permissiveness of gun laws to gain a sense of the existence and extent of gun culture in a particular geographic region.

Leisure-time Gun Use

When thinking of leisure-time gun use, the typical thought is of hunting. It turns out, however, that hunting is not the most frequent legitimate leisure-time gun activity. A survey of gun owners by the Pew Research Center found that 24% said they often or sometimes go hunting.[12] This is in comparison to the 52% of gun owners who indicated that they often or sometimes go shooting or to a gun range.[13]

Quantitative assessment and comparison of gun or shooting ranges at the state or regional level proved difficult in the absence of a central or uniform listing entity. Hunting licenses, on the other hand, can be compared across states and hence regions and therefore are used to quantify and measure hunting. According to the U.S. Fish and Wildlife Service for the year 2018, there were in excess of 37 million paid hunting license holders, as well as resident and nonresident hunting licenses, tags, permits, and stamps issued in the United States.[14] This equates to 11.30 for every 100 individuals residing in the United States during that year.[15] The only region to exceed this national rate was the Midwest. With a rate of 23.89 hunting licenses, and so on per 100 individuals, it was double the national rate.[16] The West was next with a rate of 10.12 hunting licenses per 100 individuals, followed by the South with a rate of 8.40 licenses per 100 individuals.[17] The lowest rate for the issuance of hunting licenses, tags, permits, or stamps was in the Northeast at 7.64 issuances for every 100 individuals residing in the region.[18]

The primacy of the Midwest region in this area is particularly noteworthy. It has the lowest population when compared to the other regions, but not only is its rate per 100 population higher, but its overall total number of hunting licenses issued is the highest among the regions. It is important to keep in mind that the number of hunting licenses issued does not necessarily reflect the total number of individuals engaged in hunting. It only reflects the number who took steps to acquire the legally required license. But it can be used as a proxy for hunting. The regional rank for hunting as a measure of leisure time gun use is (1) Midwest, (2) West, (3) South, and (4) Northeast.

Gun Ownership

Gun ownership is measured by the number of registered firearms. It is important to note that registration numbers only represent a portion of the total number of firearms in the United States. Some firearms are not required to be registered. Others may be required to be registered, but are not registered. To provide perspective, a report by the Congressional Research Service noted that between 1968 and 2007, the number of guns per capita in the United States increased from one gun for every two people to one gun per person.[19] To place this increase in the context of the federal firearms legislative framework discussed in chapter 2, 1968 was the year of the adoption of the GCA, and 2007 was the adoption of the National Instant Background Check System Improvements Amendment Act of 2007. The number provided in the Congressional Research Service Report includes both licit and illicit firearms. In comparison, registered firearms, which are the subject of this discussion, represent two guns for every 100 individuals.[20]

The South has long been perceived as a region where guns are a distinct part of the regional culture. Using registered firearms to represent gun ownership, six of the top ten states in terms of gun ownership were in the South.[21] Out of over 6 million registered firearms in the United States, almost half (49%) of the registered firearms in the nation were in the South. About 24% were in the West, 16% in the Midwest, and 11% in the Northeast.[22] When comparing the registered firearm percentage to the population percentage, there is an equivalence only for the Western region. Twenty-four percent of the nation's registered firearms are registered to gun owners in the West, and 24% of the nation's population resides in the West. The Midwest and the Northeast both have a population percentage that exceeds their percentage of the nation's registered firearms. The Midwest has a +5 and the Northeast a +6 population percentage point advantage over the percentage for registered firearms. For the South, the movement is in the opposite direction. There is a deficit between its percentage of the nation's population and its national firearm percentage at −11 percentage points. Or, another way to consider this is that the Southern share of the percentage of nationally registered firearms is 11 percentage points higher than its percentage of the U.S. population. The regional ranking for gun ownership, therefore, is (1) South, (2) West, (3) Midwest, and (4) Northeast.

Gun Deaths

Almost 40,000 individuals were killed by firearms in 2017.[23] This is a national firearm mortality rate of 12.20 firearm deaths per 100,000 population.[24] As with gun ownership, the South leads the nation in firearm deaths with a median rate of 17.20 firearm deaths per 100,000.[25] The West has the next highest median rate at 15.80, followed by the Midwest at 12.00.[26] The Northeast has the lowest median firearms mortality rate at 7.85.[27] Both the South and West are above the national median. It is not unexpected that the regional rankings for gun ownership and gun deaths are aligned. Gun victims are more likely to die by their own hand than by the hand of someone else. Among 2017 firearm fatalities, the Pew Research Center reported that 60% died from suicide, 37% from homicide, and the remaining 3% from other causes.[28] A study from the Harvard School of Public Health found a strong, although inexact, correlation between gun prevalence and suicide rates. The inexactness of the correlation was attributed to the influences of population density, poverty, and crime.[29]

Research has repeatedly found a correlation between the availability of guns and suicide rates, thus linking this subsection to the preceding and subsequent subsections and illustrating the interconnectedness of these cultural variables. For instance, Jehan et al. studied persons admitted to hospitals with firearm-related injuries. When comparing states with strict firearm laws to those with non-strict firearm laws, the proportion of individuals with suicidal firearm injuries was significantly lower in strict firearm law states than in non-strict firearm law states.[30] A positive association was found between household gun ownership and youth suicide. At the state level, the youth suicide rate increases by 29.6% for each 10% increase in household gun ownership.[31] Among homicides, a positive association was found to exist with household gun ownership and female non-stranger firearm homicides.[32] For gun deaths, the regional ranking is (1) South, (2) West, (3) Midwest, and (4) Northeast.

Permissiveness of Gun Laws

A commonly used metric for evaluating the permissiveness of gun laws is the Brady Campaign Scorecard.[33] The Brady Campaign to prevent gun violence evaluated and ranked the gun laws in each of the fifty states. These rankings utilized thirty-three gun policies, as well as the state firearm death rate and the state crime gun export rate. The gun policies examined included policies associated with who could carry a firearm, concealed carry rules, background checks, and so on. Each state was assigned a score and a ranking. The maximum number of points a state could receive was 100 points. The scores ranged from the −39 awarded Arizona, to the 76 awarded California. Accordingly, Arizona was ranked #1 as the most permissive gun law state, while California ranked #50 and was the least permissive gun law state.[34]

On a regional level, the West would be rated as the most permissive region in regards to gun laws with a median score of −19.[35] The states in the West had scores that ranged from Arizona's −39 to California's 76. It should be noted that while having the most permissive gun laws on a regional level, the Western region also contains the widest diversity among its states in terms of the numerical scores on the relative permissiveness of their gun laws. However, when looking at the individual state scores, 62% of the states in the Western region scored below zero. This suggests that despite a diversity which includes states with fairly restrictive gun laws, in the West, the normative gun law characteristic is permissiveness. Very close to the West in its regional score was the South, which had a median score of −18. The states in the Southern region ranged from a low score of −27, which was held by the state of Louisiana to a high of 56, which was held by the state of Maryland.

Ninety-four percent of the states in the Southern region scored below zero. Despite the Western region's one-point advantage in median scores, this increased percentage of states in the South with extremely permissive scores would counterbalance that one point, such that these two regions could be considered tied. The Midwest had a median score of 0.0 with state scores ranging from Indiana's −14.5 to Illinois' 40.5. With one half of its states at or above zero, the Midwest could be considered as either the third most permissive, or the second least permissive region in regards to gun laws. The Northeast region had the least permissive gun laws with a median score of 55. The states in the Northeast ranged from a low of −20 awarded to the state of Maine to a high of 73 awarded to the state of Connecticut. In this region, 70% of the states had scores at or above zero. For permissiveness of gun laws, the regional ranking is (1) West and South, (3) Midwest, and (4) Northeast.[36]

Regional Comparison

This section surveyed the gun culture of the four regions examining leisure-time gun activity. Gun ownership, gun deaths, and permissiveness of gun laws were examined to gain a sense of the intertwining of guns in day-to-day life in the region. Hunting was used as a proxy for leisure-time gun activity, and the issuance of licenses, permits, and so on per state was used to measure hunting. Registered firearms were used as a proxy for measuring gun owner-ship. It should be recognized that there are a significant number of firearms that are not captured in registration information, thus leaving the exact number unknown. Having a connection to gun ownership were gun deaths, including both homicide and suicide. Gun deaths were the most precise of the metrics used. This section concluded with a regional comparison of the permissiveness of gun laws using the Brady State Scorecard for state scores to obtain the regional measurements. These individual measures were used to compare regions, and a composite score was devised to facilitate an overall comparison.

Table 3.1 compares the regions across each of these four categories. The score for each region is based on the mean of their rankings in each of these four categories. With one representing the most significant immersion of guns into the regional culture and four representing the least significant, the South and the West at 1.5 and 1.75 respectively are the most identified with gun culture using these measures. The Northeast is at the opposite end of the spectrum, with an overall score of 4. Despite being three out of four, the Midwest's score at 2.5 is closer to the Southern and Western regions than it is to the Northeast.

Table 3.1   Compiled Rankings for Presence of a Supportive Regional Gun Culture

	Midwest	Northeast	South	West
Leisure-time use	1	4	3	2
Gun Ownership	3	4	1	2
Gun Deaths	3	4	1	2
Permissiveness of Gun Laws	3	4	1	1
Score	2.5	4	1.5	1.75

With the regions falling in this order along a gun culture spectrum, the question is the extent to which the school-based mass shootings of the past twenty-year period mirror this pattern. If the gun culture among the four regions can be viewed along the continuum of their scores, it could be expected that school-based mass shootings would also track this continuum. When the occurrence of school-based mass shootings is equated with the availability of guns, that expectation is particularly pronounced. Based on this analysis of regional gun culture, it could be expected that the highest number of school-based mass shootings would be in the South, followed closely by the Western region. The Midwest would be expected to rank third, with the Northeast region expected to be the site of the lowest number of school-based mass shootings. As the subsequent section will show, however, when school-based mass shooting incidents are examined within their regional and state context, the findings are more nuanced.

REGIONAL AND STATE ANALYSIS OF SCHOOL-BASED MASS SHOOTING INCIDENTS

Occurring in one out of every two states, school-based mass shootings on initial inspection appear to be a ubiquitous phenomenon. A closer examination suggests a phenomenon that is more isolated than it initially appears. Despite the wide dispersal in the occurrence of incidents, the majority of school-based mass shootings were confined to only a few states. The majority of fatalities occurred in an even smaller number of states.

Our hundred-year search going back to 1919 found forty-three school-based mass shootings, the first of which did not occur until 1940.[37] These shootings occurred in 27 different states and accounted for an overall total of 161 fatalities with 388 injuries. Nine of the states had more than one incident. For the period encompassed in the 20 years from Columbine to Santa Fe, there were 17 school-based mass shootings in 12 different states resulting in 105 fatalities and 125 injuries. These seventeen incidents represent approximately 40% of the school-based mass shootings in the past hundred years but accounted for 65% of fatalities and 33% of injuries.

While school-based mass shootings are considered a relatively rare occur-rence, the increase in fatality numbers relative to the overall number of incidents is disquieting and worthy of examination. When examining the seventeen school-based mass shootings that are the subject of this book, two-thirds of the incidents occurred in the West and the Midwest regions, and the remaining one-third in the South and Northeast. There is an inverse result with the number of fatalities. Sixty percent of the fatalities occurred in the South and Northeast. Forty percent of the fatalities occurred in the West and Midwest regions.

The largest number of school-based mass shootings were in the West, which had 35% of the school-based mass shooting incidents in the past 20 years, but just 25% of the fatalities. Twenty-nine percent of the school-based mass shootings occurred in the Midwest region, accounting for 15% of the fatalities. Twenty-four percent of the school-based mass shootings were located in the Southern region, as were 28% of the fatalities. The Northeast region was home to 12% of the school-based mass shootings but accounted for 32% of the overall fatalities.

As can be seen in most of the regions, there is a disconnect between the number of school-based mass shootings and the level of fatalities represented by those shootings. For instance, the Western region is home to one in three incidents, while the Northeast region is home to one in three fatalities. The Southern region has the greatest internal alignment in its national percentage of incidents and fatalities, with only a four percentage point gap between the two. The largest gap is found in the Northeast region, with a 20 percentage point gap. The Northeast also had the highest ratio of fatalities to incidents at 17:1. This is more than double the South, the next closet region, which has a fatality to incident ratio of 7.25:1. The West has a ratio of 4.3:1, and the Midwest is the lowest with a ratio of fatalities to incidents at 3.2:1. The varia-tion among the regional fatality to incident ratio is emblematic of differences among school-based mass shootings in the regions. This section will examine these differences. This will take place through an examination of fatalities among school-based mass shootings within regions and then at the state level.

Western Region

As indicated in table 3.1, the West has the second highest regional rating in terms of a supportive gun culture. The Western region also has the larg-est number of occurrences of school-based mass shootings during these twenty years. The thirteen states in the Western region are Alaska, Arizona, California, Colorado, Hawaii, Idaho, Montana, Nevada, New Mexico, Oregon, Utah, Washington, and Wyoming.[38] Six of the seventeen school-based mass shooting incidents occurred in the Western region with an accompanying total of twenty-six fatalities. This includes three incidents in California, one incident in Colorado, and two incidents in Washington State. The one incident in Colorado at Columbine High School in Littleton accounted for 71% of fatalities in the West. Another incident had injuries but no fatalities.[39] Perhaps corresponding to its greater diversity in gun scores, the Western region also had the greatest diversity among its perpetrators. The seven perpetrators for school-based mass shootings occurring in the West include the only African American perpetrator and one of two American Indian perpetrators.[40] They also include one of the only two perpetrators who were neither students nor former students of the targeted school. One-half of the incidents in the Western region culminated with the suicide of the perpetrator.

Colorado covers 104,100 square miles and is the eighth largest state in the nation.[41] With the highest mean altitude of any states at 6,800 feet above sea level, it has the largest number of mountains over 14,000 feet or higher.[42] By 2018, Colorado had an estimated population of 5.7 million people.[43] The one shooting in Colorado and, in fact, the worst shooting in the Western region was in Littleton, a suburb of Denver and part of the Denver-Aurora metropolitan area. On April 20, 1999, at Columbine High School in Littleton armed with explosives and weapons two white males Dylan Klebold and Eric Harris ages seventeen and eighteen respectively entered the school with multiple weapons including an Intratec TEC-DC9, 9 mm semiautomatic handgun, Hi-Point 995 or 9 mm Carbine Rifle; Savage-Springfield 67H pump-action shotgun sawed off to 26″; and a Stevens 311D 12-gauge double-barreled sawed-off shotgun 23″.[44] They killed 13 individuals before killing themselves.

The State of California encompasses 164,696 square miles making it the third largest state in terms of geographic space. California stretches 900 miles along the Pacific coast of the United States northward from the Mexican border. The nation's most populous state, by 2018 it had an estimated population of 39.6 million.[45] California's three school-based mass shootings occurred over a sixteen-year period and were responsible for a total of five fatalities. Two of these incidents occurred in the same school district less than three weeks apart. In Santee on March 5, 2001, at the Santana High School, a fifteen-year-old white male, Charles Andrew Williams, armed with a .22 caliber handgun, killed two students and injured thirteen others.[46] The second incident occurred four miles away in El Cajon at the Granite Hills High School on March 22, 2001. Jason Hoffman, an eighteen-year-old white male student, injured five with a 12-gauge shotgun. He had a .22 caliber handgun in his waistband.[47] There were no fatalities.

Following the Santana High School shooting, the school district changed its policies to require that school safety officers be assigned to only one school. At the time of the Santana High School shooting, a single officer was responsible for several campuses, and when that shooting occurred, the assigned officer for Santana High School was not initially on campus.[48] This policy change was believed at least partially responsible for the absence of fatalities in the Granite Hills High School mass shooting.[49] The mass shooting at North Park Elementary School in San Bernardino, California, on April 10, 2017, was the only shooting in the Western region where the perpetrator was not a student at the targeted school. Instead, he was the estranged husband of a teacher at the school. Cedric Anderson, a 53-year-old African American male, killed three people, including himself, and injured a fourth with a .357 caliber handgun.[50] Despite the size of the state, these three school-based mass shootings in California occurred within the same 100-mile radius.

Washington has 71,362 square miles and a 2018 estimated population of 7.4 million persons.[51] There were two school-based mass shootings in Washington. The first was on October 24, 2014, at Marysville Pilchuck High School in Marysville when Jaylen Fryberg, a fourteen-year-old American Indian male, with a .40 caliber handgun stolen from his father killed five persons including himself and injured another. The victims were his friends and cousins, whom he had invited to join him for lunch.[52] They were specifically targeted because he did not want to die alone and wanted his friends with him. The second school-based mass shooting in Washington occurred at Freeman High School (September 13, 2017) in Rockford, Washington. Rockford is on the opposite side of the state from Marysville. Armed with an AR-15 and a pistol Caleb Sharpe, a fifteen-year-old white male killed one and injured three others before he was apprehended. Only the pistol was used in the shooting since the AR-15 jammed when he tried to load it.[53]

Midwest Region

The Midwest region ranks third out of four, albeit closer to one and two, in terms of a supportive gun culture. The twelve states in the Midwest region are Illinois, Indiana, Iowa, Kansas, Michigan, Minnesota, Missouri, Nebraska, North Dakota, Ohio, South Dakota, and Wisconsin. The five school-based mass shooting incidents occurring in the Midwest region resulted in a total of sixteen fatalities. As with the Western region, school-based mass shootings were situated in three states. There were three incidents in Ohio and one each in Nebraska and Minnesota. Also, similar to the Western region, one incident was responsible for a disproportionate number of fatalities, while another incident had no fatalities Three incidents ended with the suicide of the perpetrator. Sixty-three percent ($n=16$) of the school-based mass shooting fatalities in the Midwest region were attributable to the shooting at Red Lake Senior High School in Red Lake, Minnesota (March 21, 2005).

Minnesota is 86,943 square miles with Canada on its northern border and geographically is the twelfth largest state.[54] Its 2018 estimated population of 5.6 million places it twenty-second in terms of state populations.[55] The shooting at Red Lake Senior High School occurred on the Red Lake Indian Reservation on March 21, 2005. Jeffery Weise, a 16-year-old American Indian male, stole his grandfather's 12-gauge shotgun and .40 caliber revolver. He killed ten people, including himself, and injured another seven.[56] In a pattern seen in other school-based mass shootings, the first death occurred in the perpetrator's home among their family before moving to the school. Beginning in his home, Jeffery Weise killed his grandfather and his grandfather's girlfriend. He then moved to the school, where he killed an additional seven and wounded seven before killing himself. This was the largest mass shooting in Minnesota's history.

Ohio is 44,828 square miles, and ranks thirty-fourth in terms of size.[57] With a population of 11.7 million,[58] it has twice the population of Minnesota occupying one-half the geographic space. There were three school-based mass shootings in Ohio, with a total of four fatalities. Asa Coon, a fourteen-year-old white male, armed with a .22 caliber handgun and a .38 caliber handgun, wounded four people before killing himself at Success Tech High School on October 10, 2007, in Cleveland.[59] He was the only fatality. Thirty-six miles away, on February 27, 2012, T. J. Lane, a white male seventeen-year old with a .22 caliber handgun, killed three and wounded another three at Chardon High School in Chardon before surrendering to authorities.[60] On the opposite side of the state in Middletown, James "Austin" Hancock, a fourteen-year-old white male on February 29, 2016, having stolen his grandmother's 9mm handgun brought it to Madison High School to show it off. He ended up wounding four people. There were no fatalities.[61]

The Midwest state with the lowest number of fatalities is Nebraska. It is 77,385 square miles and is the sixteenth largest state in terms of square miles.[62] On January 5, 2011, the assistant principal was targeted and killed; two others were wounded at the Millard South High School in Omaha before Robert Butler, Jr., took his own life. The eighteen-year-old white male shooter had taken a .22 caliber handgun from his father, who was a police officer in Omaha.[63]

Southern Region

The South ranked number one among regions for a supportive gun culture. The South also had the highest number of different states that were the sites of school-based mass shootings. The four school-based mass shootings in the Southern region resulted in twenty-nine fatalities. There was one incident each in Florida, Georgia, Kentucky, and Texas. The shooting at Heritage High School in Conyers, Georgia (May 20, 1999), which occurred a month following Columbine, left six wounded but had no fatalities. On the other end of the spectrum, the school-based mass shooting at Marjory Stoneman Douglas High School in Parkland, Florida (February 14, 2018), was responsible for almost 60% of the fatalities in the Southern region. The shooting at Santa Fe High School in Santa Fe, Texas (May 18, 2018), was responsible for another 34% of the fatalities in this region. In other words, two of the four schools that were sites of school-based mass shootings in the South contained 94% of the fatalities for that region. The South was unique among the regions in that none of its school-based mass shooting incidents ended with the perpetrator's suicide.

The state of Florida is 59,988 square miles and is ranked twenty-third in size.[64] In 2018, it had a population of 21,299,325. On February 14, 2018, armed with an AR-15 rifle, Nikolas Cruz, a nineteen-year-old white male student, killed seventeen and wounded another seventeen at the Marjory Stoneman Douglas High School in Parkland, Florida. He was later apprehended.[65] Three months later, on May 18, 2018, at the Santa Fe High School in Santa Fe, Texas, ten persons were killed and another thirteen injured. Dimitrios Pagourtzis, a seventeen-year-old white male, used his father's 12-gauge Remington 870 shotgun, and also had a Rossi .38 caliber snub-nosed revolver.[66]

The first school-based mass shooting in 2018 was in Benton, Kentucky, with a 2018 estimated population of 4,469. Gabriel Ross Parker, a fifteen-year-old white male, took his stepfather's 9 mm semiautomatic pistol as well as a hunting knife. The hunting knife was in case he ran out of bullets.[67] He killed two and wounded eighteen at Marshall County High School. The first school-based mass shooting in the Southern region was exactly one month after Columbine, in Conyers, Georgia, at Heritage High School. On May 20, 1999, T. J. Soloman, a white fifteen-year-old male, wounded six students with a .22 caliber rifle and a .357 handgun.[68] There were no fatalities. While at the time of this shooting, authorities would not indicate the source of the weapons, his friends told reporters that a range of hunting weapons had been seen in his home.[69]

Northeast Region

The smallest number of school-based mass shootings occurred in the Northeast. The Northeast region had two school-based mass shootings, but at thirty-four fatalities, it had the highest number of fatalities. Sandy Hook Elementary School in Newtown, Connecticut (December 14, 2012), accounted for 84% of those fatalities. The shooting at West Nickel Mines School in Nickel Mines, Pennsylvania (October 2, 2006), was responsible for the remaining 16% of fatalities in the Northeast region and ranked number six overall in fatalities from school-based mass shootings. Both of these incidents ended in the suicide of the perpetrator.

On December 14, 2012, Adam Lanza, a twenty-year-old white male, first killed his mother then went to Sandy Hook Elementary School, where he killed twenty children and six adults, wounding two others before killing himself. He was armed with multiple weapons, including an AR-15, a 10 mm Glock, and a 9 mm Sig Sauer. His mother had been making straw purchases of guns for him.[70] Six years earlier Charles C. Roberts, a 32-year-old white male, walked into the West Nickle Mines School in an Amish community on October 2, 2006, with a 9 mm semiautomatic pistol, two shotguns, a stun gun, two knives, two cans of gunpowder, and 600 rounds of ammunition looking for female victims.[71] He tied up his victims before shooting them. Charles C. Roberts killed five and wounded six before killing himself.

Regional Comparison

There are similarities and distinct differences among the regions in terms of the characteristics associated with the school-based mass shootings occurring in their geographic space. With the exception of the Southern region, the regional pattern was a single incident with double-digit fatalities and other low fatality incidents. The South, however, had two incidents with double-digit fatalities occurring three months apart. A slight regional variation was found for the age of the perpetrators. Age appears to be connected to the number of fatalities.

While he is included in table 3.2, if Cedric Anderson, the 53-year-old shooter who in all likelihood was engaged in an act of domestic violence at a school, is excluded from the age range of the Western region perpetrators, then the West has the same age range of fourteen to eighteen as the Midwest. Even with his inclusion, what is noticeable about the West and the Midwest is the relative youth of their perpetrators. Forty-two percent ($n=12$) of the school-based mass shooters in the West and Midwest were fifteen years of age or younger. This compares to 33% ($n=6$) of those in the South and Northeast. Along with its youthful perpetrators, the West and Midwest are

Table 3.2   Regional Characteristics of School-Based Mass Shootings

Region	Shooter Suicide (%)	Incidents with No Fatalities (%)	Shooter Age Range	Number of Incidents	Number of Fatalities
West	50	17	14–53	6	26
Midwest	20	20	14–18	5	16
South	0	25	15–19	4	29
Northeast	100	0	20–32	2	34

both characterized by relatively high numbers of incidents, but low fatalities. The South and the Northeast, on the other hand, are characterized by lower numbers of incidents, but higher fatalities. The South and the Northeast are also characterized by the fact that they both are on the extreme end of the range in regards to shooters who committed suicide. The Northeast was the only region where all of the perpetrators committed suicide. Standing in direct contrast to the Northwest, none of the shooters in the Southern region committed suicide.

CONCLUSION

This chapter explored the interplay between the existence of a regional gun culture and the school-based mass shootings that occur in that region. The Southern region was found to have the most supportive gun culture, followed closely by the Western region. The Midwest was third, although it scored closer to the Western region than it did to with the Northeast, which was found to have the least supportive gun culture. Connections were found between the gun culture score of a region and some aspects of school-based mass shooting incidents in that region.

As may be expected, the Northeast, the region with the least supportive gun culture, is the region with the lowest number of school-based mass shooting incidents. What may not be expected is that it is also the region with the highest number of fatalities. The Northeast was also the only region that had fatalities in all incidents. The Southern region, which had the most supportive gun culture had the second lowest number of shootings, but the second highest number of fatalities. The South, Midwest, and West each had one incident with no fatalities in their region. The Western region, with the second highest supportive gun culture rating, had the largest number of incidents but the third lowest number of fatalities. Number of incidents and number of fatalities seem to operate in an inverse manner. The Midwest, with the third-lowest score, had the second highest number of shooting incidents but the lowest number of fatalities. School-based mass shooting fatalities in the Midwest were less than half ($n=34$) the number of fatalities in the Northeast, which had the highest. The Midwest fatalities were approximately 62% ($n=26$) of these in the West, which was the next closest region in terms of fatalities.

The question is, why? What do these things suggest? As was noted at the beginning of this chapter, relationships have been found between mass shootings and both permissive gun laws and higher rates of gun ownership. It is not as clear cut for school-based mass shootings. The West ranked highest in the permissiveness of its gun laws, and it did have the most school-based mass shooting incidents. But it ranked second from the bottom in terms of fatalities. The South ranked highest in gun ownership and was second from the bottom in regards to the number of incidents, but second from the top in regards to the number of fatalities.

A hint may lie in a region's leisure-time use of firearms. As illustrated in table 3.1, the regions ranked in order: Midwest, West, South, and Northeast in regards to their leisure time use of firearms. The top two regions in this category, Midwest and West, had the highest number of incidents but ranked the reverse in fatalities. In contrast, the Northeast region ranked at the bottom in terms of leisure-time use of firearms. It had the lowest number of incidents but the highest number of fatalities. The South ranked just above the Northeast with the second lowest number of incidents, and the second highest number of fatalities. A key aspect that emerges when looking at a region's leisure-time firearm use and school-based mass shootings is that the higher a region's leisure-time gun use, the lower its fatalities from school-based mass shootings, both in total and as a function of a fatality to incident ratio. This is a counterintuitive finding. It is just as counterintuitive that the Northeast with the least supportive gun culture would have the largest number of fatalities. However, the connection between leisure-time gun use and the high number of incidents does connect with Vizzard's linkage between homicide as a spontaneous activity and the availability of guns (*supra*).

This suggests that a supportive gun culture does play a role in school-based mass shootings, but that the school-based mass shooting phenomenon also has other factors at work that influence outcomes. The next chapter will add selected socioeconomic factors for consideration in this analysis.

NOTES

1. (Lemieux 2014).
2. A macro-level analysis compared the United States to twenty-four other developed countries.
3. (Felson and Pare 2010).
4. (Vizzard 2015).
5. (Towers et al. 2015).
6. (Reeping et al. 2019).
7. (Zimmerman and Fridel 2019).
8. (Siegel et al. 2019).
9. (U.S. Census Bureau 2018).
10. The percentages were calculated based on data obtained from the U.S. Census (U.S. Census Bureau 2018). For the list of state groups see https://www2.census.gov /geo/pdfs/maps-data/maps/reference/us_regdiv.pdf.

11. The percentages were calculated based on data from obtained from the U.S. Census (U.S. Census Bureau 2018). For the list of state groupings see https://www2 .census.gov/geo/pdfs/maps-data/maps/reference/us_regdiv.pdf.

12. (Pew Research Center 2017).

13. (Pew Research Center 2017).

14. (U.S. Fish and Wildlife Service n.d.).

15. Data from (U.S. Census Bureau 2018) and (U.S. Fish and Wildlife Service n.d.) were used to calculate the rate.

16. Data from (U.S. Census Bureau 2018) and (U.S. Fish and Wildlife Service n.d.) were used to calculate the rate.

17. Data from (U.S. Census Bureau 2018) and (U.S. Fish and Wildlife Service n.d.) were used to calculate the rate.

18. Data from (U.S. Census Bureau 2018) and (U.S. Fish and Wildlife Service n.d.) were used to calculate the rate.

19. (Krause 2012). This was based on a self-report survey from the National Institute of Justice, and data from the U.S. Department of Justice, Bureau of Alcohol, Tobacco, Firearms, and Explosives.

20. Calculation based on data provided in the following data sources: (ATF 2019); (U.S. Census Bureau 2018).

21. (ATF 2019).

22. Data from (ATF 2019) was consolidated into regions for calculation.

23. Data Source: (CDC, National Center for Health Statistics 2019).

24. Identified using data from (CDC, National Center for Health Statistics 2019) and 2017 population data from (U.S. Census Bureau 2018).

25. Identified using data from (CDC, National Center for Health Statistics 2019) and 2017 population data from (U.S. Census Bureau 2018).

26. Identified using data from (CDC, National Center for Health Statistics 2019) and 2017 population data from (U.S. Census Bureau 2018).

27. Identified using data from (CDC, National Center for Health Statistics 2019) and 2017 population data from (U.S. Census Bureau 2018).

28. (Gramlich 2019), citing Centers for Disease Control and Prevention.

29. (Harvard School of Public Health 2008).

30. (Jehan et al. 2018). This study used the 2011 National Inpatient Sample Database to examine the relationship between state firearm legislative and firearm injuries.

31. (Knopov et al. 2019).

32. (Seigel and Rothman 2016).

33. (The Brady Campaign to Prevent Gun Violence 2015).

34. (The Brady Campaign to Prevent Gun Violence 2015).

35. The regional scores for permissiveness of gun laws were calculated using the Brady scorecard dataset (The Brady Campaign to Prevent Gun Violence 2015).

36. Due to the tie, there was no second place ranking.

37. (Lane and Flowers 2019). Unless otherwise indicated, all numerical and statistical data presented came from that dataset.

38. (U.S. Census Bureau n.d.).

39. The definition used for school-based mass shooting in this research speaks to four or more persons killed or injured. Therefore a mass shooting incident could have injuries but no fatalities.
40. It was decided to use the census terminology when referring to racial and ethnic designations.
41. (Netstate.com 2016).
42. (Netstate.com 2016).
43. (U.S. Census Bureau 2018).
44. In addition, they wounded another twenty-one people. (History.com 2019).
45. (U.S. Census Bureau 2018).
46. (Purdum 2001).
47. (Sterngold 2001).
48. (Sterngold 2001).
49. (Sterngold 2001).
50. (Hamasaki and Simon 2017).
51. (U.S. Census Bureau 2018).
52. (Kutner 2015).
53. (CBS NEWS AP 2017).
54. (Netstate.com 2017).
55. (U.S. Census Bureau 2018).
56. (Enger 2015).
57. (Netstate.com 2017).
58. (U.S. Census Bureau 2018).
59. (Maag and Urbina 2007).
60. (Plain Dealer Staff 2019).
61. (Hagman 2016).
62. (Netstate.com 2017).
63. (Welch 2011).
64. (Netstate.com 2017).
65. (Levenson and Sterling 2018).
66. (Hanna et al. 2018).
67. (Sayers and Wolfson 2018).
68. (Pressley 1999).
69. (Pressley 1999).
70. (Lupica 2013).
71. (Kocieniewski and Gately 2006).

Chapter 4

School-Based Mass Shootings and the Socioeconomics of Place

INTRODUCTION

Seventy-two percent (*n=17*) of school-based mass shootings in the past twenty years have happened in nonurban areas. School-based mass shootings disproportionately occur in either rural or suburban jurisdictions. This is the first important geographic fact of note. Despite being an unrelated sociological phenomenon, school shootings are often erroneously compared to or juxtaposed with urban crime.[1] There is a prevalent misperception that urban areas are the principal repositories of crime and that "bad things" don't happen in "nice" suburban or rural neighborhoods. This is not to suggest that shootings in or near schools do not occur in urban areas. Shootings of all types are far too common in those jurisdictions but are beyond the scope of this book. The misperception, or rather the erroneous expectation of who is potentially vulnerable, can hinder the search for solutions and public policy responses.

With fewer than two out of every ten school-based mass shootings occurring in urban areas, it illustrates that this particular phenomenon is associated with a type of community normally thought of as sheltered from crime. These communities, moreover, tend to be located in areas that are not home to the vast majority of people in this country. Urban areas comprise approximately 3% of the U.S. land mass but are home to more than 80% of the nation's population.[2] The remaining 97% of the nation's landmass is inhabited by less than 20% of the nation's population.[3] These areas are usually sparsely populated and far from urban centers.

The reverse side of the question as to why school-based mass shootings do not typically occur in urban areas is the question of why school-based mass shootings are more likely to occur in suburban or rural areas. Are

57

there some influencing characteristics associated with the geographic space within which these incidents occur? The examination of socioeconomic aspects of place, of the geographic space in which school-based mass shootings occur, is the focus of this chapter. This chapter begins with the locality or jurisdiction itself: the city, town, or unincorporated area whose name is sometimes more recognizable than the name of the school where the mass shooting occurred. That geographic space will be used to explore the intersection between population size and the fatalities and injuries resulting from the school-based mass shootings in a particular locale. From there, the chapter moves to an examination of school neighborhoods or communities. It is important to distinguish between several terms as they are used in this chapter. Jurisdiction refers to the city, town, or unincorporated area. It is the locality within which an incident occurred. Community or neighborhood refers to that subsection of the jurisdiction immediately surrounding the school.

A look at neighborhoods is important when studying school-based mass shootings. These shootings do not simply take place inside a school or on the school grounds. They also take place within the environment of their surrounding community. This chapter examines the characteristics of local school communities in an effort to provide identifiable factors for recognizing the types of communities that are most likely to be vulnerable to these occurrences. A case study overview of communities that are the site of outlier incidents will be undertaken. At the conclusion, a multilevel comparison will take place. Outlier communities will be compared to each other to identify whether there are shared characteristics. They will also be compared to the other neighborhoods in which school-based mass shootings occur to address the question of whether there are distinguishing socioeconomic characteristics between the neighborhoods where the school-based mass shootings generate high fatalities and those with low fatalities. The comparison to national averages is designed to indicate whether or not socioeconomic characteristics are identifiable distinguishing neighborhood factors.

JURISDICTION CHARACTERISTICS

This section explores whether the primacy of nonurban jurisdictions in relation to the number of incidents also holds for the level of fatalities and injuries resulting from those incidents. Subsequent sections will delve down into the specific neighborhood or communities within those jurisdictions, that immediately surround the school. For organizing purposes, the jurisdictions in this section are discussed within regions. This supports a continuing look across chapters at any regional characteristics that emerge.

The U.S. Census Bureau primarily uses residential population, density, land use, and distance in its definition of urban. Determinations of urban or rural are made at the block level. A block must have a population density of 1,000 persons per square mile to be considered urban. But, assuming the density requirement is met, additional factors come into play in determining urbanization. An urbanized area must have at least 50,000 people, while an urban cluster has between 2,500 and 50,000. The Census Bureau defines rural as all people, housing, and territory that is not included in an urban area or urban cluster.[4] As a result of this definition, rural areas can include a range of settlement types such as remote and sparsely populated areas, "large-lot" housing subdivisions existing on the fringes of urban areas, or densely settled small cities or towns.[5]

Suburbs, while not expressly described by the Census Bureau in this context, exist for all practical purposes in the space between urban and rural. They have a larger population than rural areas and a smaller population than urban areas. Their land-use requirements are also different. Urban, suburban, and rural communities can also be described by a variety of socioeconomic, lifestyle, or cultural factors. Among the most obvious example, farms are found in rural areas. Rural areas have also seen a decline in the number of employed adults ages 25–54, while urban and suburban communities have seen an increase.[6] In suburban communities, the incidence of poverty has risen faster than in urban or rural communities.[7]

Population size is used in this section to examine the differences among school-based mass shooting outcomes and the type of jurisdiction. Residential population and population density are used to take a closer look at the characterization of these jurisdictions. The residential population is the number of persons that reside in the jurisdiction. But that number alone provides an incomplete picture of the interplay between population and geography. For instance, two jurisdictions can both have populations of 25,000 people. However, in one jurisdiction, the population may be spread over 10 square miles, and in another jurisdiction, the population may be spread over 100 square miles. Population density is the measurement used to reflect that difference. It refers to the number of people per square mile. Population density reveals the difference between a jurisdiction where an individual family resides on a multi-acre farm and one where they reside in a high-rise multifamily dwelling. It should be noted that since population density is a mathematical construct, for very small jurisdictions, the population density figure can exceed the number of people who live in the jurisdiction.

Two-thirds (*n=6*) of the school-based mass shootings in the West occurred in suburban or rural jurisdictions. The Western region included one shooting in Colorado (Littleton), three in California (Santee, El Cajon, and San Bernardino), and two in Washington (Marysville, and Rockford).

Except for the two localities in Washington, the jurisdictions in the West typically had higher population densities than found in the other regions (see table 4.1). The West had the largest number of incidents of school-based mass shootings, but the second lowest overall average per incident for fatalities as well as for fatalities and injuries combined at 4.33 and 11.67, respectively.

Sixty percent (*n*=5) of the school-based mass shootings in the Midwest region occurred in suburban or rural jurisdictions. Two-thirds (*n*=3) of the urban jurisdictions that were the location of school-based mass shootings in the nation were situated in the Midwest. The Midwest region included one shooting in Minnesota (Red Lake), three in Ohio (Cleveland, Chardon, and Middleton), and one in Nebraska (Omaha). Cleveland and Omaha were the largest urban jurisdictions in the nation that were the site of school-based mass shootings. The Midwest contains the sole jurisdiction that was among the top five school-based mass shooting incidents, where the median household income was below the national median household income. School-based shootings in the Midwest region had the lowest average both in fatalities alone, as well as fatalities and injuries combined at 3.20 and 7.20, respectively.

Seventy-five percent (*n*=4) of the school-based mass shootings in the South occurred in suburban jurisdictions, with 25% occurring in a rural jurisdiction. This region had the most state diversity, with incidents spread across four states: Georgia (Conyers), Kentucky (Benton), Florida (Parkland), and Texas (Santa Fe). The population and density of these jurisdictions were lower than most of the jurisdictions in the West and Midwest. The South ranked three out of four in the number of school-based mass shooting incidents. However, it had the second highest fatality average, and the highest average for fatalities and injuries combined at 7.25 and 20.75, respectively. Two of the school-based mass shooting incidents in the Southern region were among the top five school-based mass shooting incidents in terms of fatalities.

The Northeast region was the site of two school-based mass shootings. As with the South, none were in an urban jurisdiction. One jurisdiction was suburban, and the other one was rural. The two states in the Northeast were Pennsylvania (Nickel Mines) and Connecticut (Newtown). Nickel Mines, which has been estimated to have a population as low as thirty-five individuals, is too small to be recorded by the Census Bureau. The West Nickel Mines School drew its student population from several communities, not just Nickel Mines. For these reasons, the census information on the surrounding area of Bart Township is used. The Northeast had the lowest number of school-based mass shooting incidents. Conversely, it had the highest average for fatalities

Table 4.1   School-Based Mass Shooting Localities: Income and Population Comparison

Region	Jurisdiction and Year	Residential Population	Population Density	Fatalities	Injuries
West	Littleton, Colorado (1999)	41,297	2,984.8	15	21
	Santee, California (2001)	53,346	3,982.7	2	13
	El Cajon, California (2001)	95,294	6,510.6	0	5
	Marysville, Washington (2014)	64,904	2,902.5	5	1
	Rockford, Washington (2017)	477	691.2	1	3
	San Bernardino, California (2017)	216,995	3,546.0	3	1
Midwest	Red Lake, Minnesota (2005)	1,430	703.0	10	7
	Cleveland, Ohio (2007)	440,358	5,107.2	1	4
	Omaha, Nebraska (2011)	452,663	3,217.9	2	2
	Chardon, Ohio (2012)	5,166	1,124.0	3	3
	Middleton, Ohio (2016)	48,819	1,859.6	0	4
South	Conyers, Georgia (1999)	8,489	907.3	0	6
	Benton, Kentucky (2018)	4,469	1,007.4	2	18
	Parkland, Florida (2018)	30,000	1,943.4	17	17
	Santa Fe, Texas (2018)	12,222	713.1	10	13
Northeast	Nickel Mines, Pennsylvania (2006)	3,025	185.3	6	5
	Newtown, Connecticut (2012)	28,042	478.0	28	2

and the second highest average for fatalities and injuries combined at 17.00 and 20.50, respectively.

Residential population and population density are shown in table 4.1 for each jurisdiction that was the site of a school-based mass shooting along with shooting fatalities and injuries. Population was found to be correlated with fatalities from school-based mass shootings. A weak relationship between population density and fatalities was found. However, it is stronger than the relationship between residential population and fatalities.[8] The relationship identified, in both instances, was an inverse one, which is consistent with the patterns to be described below.

It is surprising that when it comes to school-based mass shootings, the major population centers are found in the West and Midwest. The two jurisdictions with the largest residential populations, Omaha, Nebraska, and Cleveland, Ohio, are located in the Midwest. The third largest jurisdiction, San Bernardino, California, is located in the West. Those were not the jurisdictions that had the high-fatality school-based mass shooting incidents, however. Sixty-seven percent ($n=105$) of all fatalities occurred in 24% ($n=17$) of the jurisdictions. Specifically, they occurred in those jurisdictions with a residential population ranging from the 12,222 of Santa Fe, Texas, to the 41,297 of Littleton, Colorado. This suggests a low to mid-range residential population within which fatalities appear to peak. The other jurisdictions included in this group are Parkland, Florida, and Newtown, Connecticut. As can be seen in table 4.1, this population range includes every jurisdiction with double-digit fatalities, except Red Lake, Minnesota.

The picture is slightly different when population density or the number of persons per square mile is examined. Population density and fatalities tend to operate inversely, with one increasing while the other decreases. Fifty-two percent ($n=105$) of fatalities occurred in 29% ($n=17$) of the jurisdictions. Those jurisdictions were the bottom five jurisdictions in terms of population density. The jurisdiction with the highest population density of the bottom five density jurisdictions, Santa Fe, Texas, had a density of 713.1 individuals. As can be seen in table 4.1, these five low population density jurisdictions included three of the five jurisdictions with double-digit fatalities. They were Newtown, Connecticut, Red Lake, Minnesota, and Santa Fe, Texas. Santa Fe, Texas, which had the top limit for population density in this grouping, had the bottom limit in terms of its residential population. Rockford, Washington, had the second highest density among the bottom five at 691.2 persons per square mile and is one of those jurisdictions whose residential population was so small, that it was exceeded by its population density. The jurisdiction with the lowest population density, Nickel Mines, Pennsylvania, ranked number six in terms of fatalities. This does suggest that the primacy of suburban and rural areas for school-based mass shootings holds not only for the number of incidents that occur but also for the resulting level of fatalities and injuries.

SOCIOECONOMICS AND NEIGHBORHOOD

This section looks at the neighborhood within which a school is located to identify its particular socioeconomic characteristics. It is the geographic space of the community that is the focal point and not the incident. The initial issue was how to define the geographic space that is the community, or the neighborhood, surrounding the school for purposes of measurement. There were four options: the entire jurisdiction, zip code area, census tract, or block group. Block groups and census tracts were deemed to be too narrow, and the entire jurisdiction was larger than desired. The goal was to look at the immediate school community. For the purpose of this study, it was decided to use the postal zip code to define the school neighborhood. Postal zip codes encompass a larger area than a block group or census tract and are thus more inclusive of a school's population. Space considerations prevent a full examination of all possible descriptive factors. Discussion is therefore limited to selected characteristics in the areas of population, labor force participation, education, income, housing, and households.

Residential population and density were discussed in regards to the overall jurisdiction. At the community level, population factors examined include median age, and race/ethnicity. Since the information being used is census data, the race designations provided in this section are those utilized by the U.S. Census Bureau. It should be noted that the percentages for race are slightly less than 100% since they do not include those who indicated more than one race or those who choose not to indicate a race. As an ethnicity, Hispanic/Latino identification co-occurs with race, and therefore its percentage should not be added to race.[9] Labor force participation includes the percentage of the population over the age of sixteen, either working or looking for work.

Education looks at the highest level of education completed by those twenty-five years of age and older in the community. The categories are completion of 5th–8th grade, 9th–12th grade but not graduated from high school, high school diploma or equivalency, and bachelor's degree or higher. Income looks at median household income. The national median household income for each incident year is used as the baseline for comparison. The median household income for the relevant community (whether school neighborhood, locality, or state) in the year of the incident was compared to the national median household income for that same year.[10] This comparison avoided the necessity of using inflation-adjusted figures. The distance from each jurisdiction's median household income to the baseline (national median household income for the corresponding year) was measured to identify the extent to which the jurisdiction's median diverged from the baseline, as well as the direction of that divergence. The resulting measurement is alternatively described as the extent of divergence or income variance. As may be expected, there is a relationship between the highest education level in a community and the median household income in that community.

The final two categories examined are housing and households. Housing looks at the number and type of housing units. Specifically, it looks at the percentage of housing units that are owner-occupied as distinct from those occupied by renters. Housing also includes the percentage of units that are vacant.

Owner-occupied housing signals permanence and residential stability. High levels of vacant housing units often signal a community in transition or turmoil. Households begin with the percentage of households in the community that are family households (as distinct from single individuals, or unrelated individuals). It also includes the percentage of households that include an individual under the age of eighteen, and the percentage of households that include an individual over the age of sixty-five. The review of households concludes with a look at household size and family size, using the average number of people for each.

The description of these characteristics will frequently involve the median. Median is the value that is in the middle. It is the type of average most frequently used in the presentation of census data. It is often selected because it is not as susceptible to extreme divergences as the mean. Exactly one-half of the values fall above the median, and one-half fall below the median. The seventeen communities containing a school that suffered a mass shooting frequently fell disproportionately on one side of the national median or the other, rather than dispersing evenly on both sides. This indicates a commonality in some aspects among these communities that is not different from the nation's communities as a whole.

There were two principal areas where the communities came closest to an equal distribution on both sides of the national median household income. The first was in regards to median household income. Fifty-nine percent ($n=17$) of the communities were above the median, the remaining 41% below the median. However, 80% ($n=5$) of the school communities with double-digit school shooting fatalities were above the national median in regards to household income, indicating a propensity for higher fatalities to cluster in more affluent neighborhoods. The second area where the communities approached an equal distribution was persons aged sixteen and older who were employed. In this case, the distribution was the same as with median household income. Fifty-nine percent ($n=17$) were above the national median household income, and 41% were below.

Uneven distributions around the national median were found in other areas. However, the nature of the imbalance was one that pointed to school communities that, on the whole, were more advantaged than the national norm. For example, using the other labor force participation indicator, the percentage of individuals looking for work, 65% ($n=17$) of these communities had a lower percentage of persons looking for work than the national median. This suggests that the communities where school-based mass shootings occurred on the aggregate were more likely to have low unemployment levels. Although the unemployment level in slightly more than one-third ($n=17$) of these communities was above the national median, they had relatively fewer people living in poverty in their communities. Only 12% ($n=17$) of the school communities had a higher percentage of individuals living in poverty than the national median. Turning to a measure of neighborhood stability, only 18% (*n=17*) of the school communities exceeded the national median housing vacancy levels.

OUTLIERS OR PREDICTORS: CASE STUDY EXAMINATION OF HIGH-FATALITY NEIGHBORHOODS

This chapter seeks to explore the connection between the socioeconomic characteristics of a community and the school-based mass shooting incidents occurring in that community.

Figure 4.1 shows the fatalities for each school-based mass shooting incident in chronological order from the April 20, 1999, shooting at Columbine High School through the May 18, 2018 shooting at Santa Fe High School. The trendline in figure 4.1 illustrates the upward progression in fatalities over time. Also illustrated in figure 4.1 are six incidents that initially appear to be responsible for the disproportionate number of fatalities in this period. It is important to note that each of the outlier incidents identified in figure 4.1 were either in the low-mid range residential population grouping or the low population density grouping or both, as discussed in the previous section.

Examination of the differences pre- and post-Columbine suggests that the explanation for the disproportionate increase in aggregate fatalities is

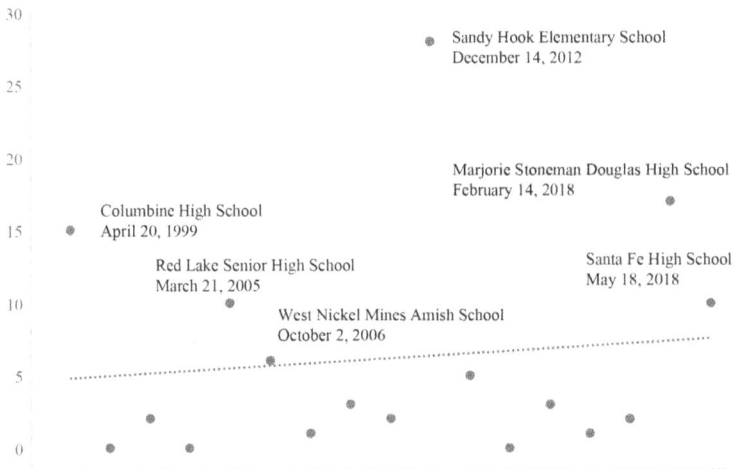

Figure 4.1   School-Based Mass Shooting Fatalities from Columbine to Santa Fe. *Source*: Figure created by authors.

not entirely attributable to increased fatalities per incident. Instead, it is also due to an increase in what initially appears to be outlier incidents. It can be argued that these incidents are not necessarily outliers. Rather, they can also be considered as predictive of an emerging pattern or, more specifically, as forerunners. Whether they are outliers, predictors, or forerunners, they have value for an in-depth examination and, as such, are used as the linchpin for our study of the connection between socioeconomic factors associated with geographic space and school-based mass shootings.

This section presents a discussion of six school communities located in the following jurisdictions: Littleton (Colorado), Red Lake (Minnesota), West Nickel Mines/Bart Township (Pennsylvania), Newtown (Connecticut), Parkland (Florida), and Santa Fe (Texas). If looking at the regional dispersal, the West and the Midwest each have one high-fatality neighborhood, while the South and the Northeast each have two. All of the incidents which occurred in the Northeast placed above the trendline. A brief overview of each incident will be provided for background information and to highlight unique community or regional characteristics. A more detailed analysis of the perpetrators of these incidents will be provided in a subsequent chapter. The focal point of this section is the characteristics of the neighborhoods immediately surrounding the target schools. Each of these communities is unique in a way that adds to the understanding of this phenomenon. Simultaneously many of these communities have common characteristics. Table 4.2 provides a summary of the selected socioeconomic characteristics of these communities.

Littleton, Colorado: Columbine High School

It was supposed to be a bombing. The bombing was meant to rival the Oklahoma City Bombing that had occurred four years earlier on April 19, 1995.[11] On Tuesday, April 20, 1999, two propane tanks had been placed in the school and were scheduled to detonate at 11:17 a.m. Eric Harris and Dylan Klebold, both white males, aged eighteen and seventeen respectively, had spent a year planning their attack. The attack was initially planned for the previous day, on the anniversary of the Oklahoma City Bombing.[12] It was delayed when their ammunition seller, a local drug dealer, was late.[13] When the bombs failed to detonate, they entered the school at 11:19 a.m. and began randomly shooting. Armed with a combination of weapons, they fired a total of 188 shots in approximately 49 minutes. Twelve students and one teacher were killed, and another twenty-one persons were injured before Harris and Klebold killed themselves.[14] First classified as a hostage event, the resulting delay in the entry of law enforcement personnel resulted in the teacher bleeding to death.[15]

Table 4.2 Comparison of High-Fatality School Neighborhoods

	Columbine High School 1999	Red Lake Senior High School 2005	West Nickel Mines Amish School 2006	Sandy Hook Elementary School 2012	Marjorie Stoneman Douglas High School	Santa Fe High School
Income Variance from National Median ($)	22,786	-21,877	-2,951	90,877	58,279	11,449
Median Age (years)	36.1	22.6	27.7	41.3	39.5	40
Race/Ethnicity						
White (%)	90.5	1.8	98.7	94.3	79.4	92
Asian (%)	2.4	—	0.1	2.7	7.2	0.3
Black/African American (%)	1.4	0.3	0.5	1.0	8.8	0.2
American Indian/ Alaskan Na (%)	0.8	97.6	0.1		—	0.9
Hispanic (%)					15.7	14.4
Labor Force Participation (%)	72.5	55.1	66.8	73.4	68.2	58.9
Unemployed (%)	1.6	11.5	0.6	6.8	3.4	3.7
Education: Highest Level						
5th–8th grade (%)	—	—	26.4	—	—	—
9th–12th grade (%)	—	32.3	—	—	—	—
High School Dipl./ Equvlncy. (%)	95	31	53	95	96	88
Bachelor's degree or higher (%)	40.5	3.4	0.2	53.9	56	11.2
Below Poverty Level (%)	3.2	31.2	13	4.8	4.5	4
Housing						
Owner-occupied (%)	74.4	69.3	72.3	90	80	94.2
Renters (%)	25.6	30.7	27.7	10	20	5.8
Vacant (%)	2.8	6	4	6	6	20

Table 4.2 Comparison of High-Fatality School Neighborhoods (*Continued*)

	Columbine High School 1999	Red Lake Senior High School 2005	West Nickel Mines Amish School 2006	Sandy Hook Elementary School 2012	Marjorie Stoneman Douglas High School	Santa Fe High School
Households						
Family (%)	67	79	83	79	85	79
Persons under eighteen (%)	34	63	40.3	45	52	39
Persons over sixty-five (%)	16.4	14	27	22.9	16	23.1
Average Household size (number of people)	2.47	3.45	3.59	2.3	3.08	2.83
Average Family size (number of people)	3.03	3.76	4.02	3.3	3.35	3.8
Fatalities	15	10	6	28	17	10

Harris and Klebold acquired their weapons in a variety of ways. An eighteen-year-old classmate bought two shotguns and a semiautomatic carbine in a straw purchase for them at a Gun Show. At the time, they were seventeen and were too young to purchase the weapons themselves. The purchaser believed they wanted the weapons for hunting.[16] Colorado was a state with a strong hunting ethos. In 1999, there were 827,700 resident hunting licenses issued for the state of Colorado.[17] To place this in context, with approximately 3.2 million people who were eighteen years of age or older, this was the equivalent to one hunting license for every four adults. Subsequently, Eric Harris purchased a TEC-DC9 from a second individual. That seller later served six years in prison for selling the gun to an underage individual.[18]

The community within which this incident occurred presented as an affluent stable community. Not only was the median household income for this community $22,786 higher than the national median household income that year, but it was also $13,000 higher than the median household income for the city of Littleton within which this community was located. Because violent crime is often erroneously associated with inner cities, poverty, and minority communities, the mass shooting at Columbine forced a reexamination of those traditional assumptions.

Red Lake, Minnesota: Red Lake Senior High School

Jeffery Weise, a sixteen-year-old Native American male, lived with his grandfather. He had studied the Columbine shooting, and he had also planned his attack. On Monday, March 21, 2005, he killed his grandfather, a tribal police officer, and his grandfather's girlfriend at home. He then took his grandfather's department-issued 12-gauge shotgun, 40-caliber handgun, and his ballistic vest. After driving his grandfather's police cruiser to Red Lake Senior High School, he entered the building firing at approximately 2:49 p.m. He continued firing through a hallway and in a classroom. Jeffrey Weise killed five students as well as a teacher and an unarmed security guard, wounding ten others. When confronted with the police, he went into a classroom and killed himself. At the time of the shooting, Jeffrey Weise was not a student at Red Lake as he had been placed in home-based schooling due to infractions of school rules. He was the only non-white perpetrator in this grouping of high-fatality incidents. It is worth noting that the non-white perpetrator percentage in this outlier group was 16.7% (*n=6*), which is very close to the non-white percentage for the entire group of seventeen school-based mass shooting incidents at 17.6%.

Red Lake Nation, home of the Chippewa Indians, in Red Lake, Minnesota, was a very different community than was found in Littleton, Colorado. The Red Lake Reservation is considered a closed reservation; as a result, very few nonmembers live on the reservation.[19] Red Lake was the only jurisdiction with double-digit fatalities that had a negative divergence from the national household median income. The immediate school community had a -$21,877 extent of divergence. But it was still slightly more than $1,000 higher than the jurisdiction as a whole. The jurisdiction of Red Lake itself had the lowest negative divergence of any of the other seventeen jurisdictions. The neighborhood surrounding Red Lake Senior High School also had the youngest median age for its population at 22.6 years old, in comparison to the other five neighborhoods in this case study group.[20]

Nickel Mines (Bart Township), Pennsylvania: West Nickel Mines School

Charles C. Roberts had been stockpiling the supplies he would use for months, indicating that he too had been planning. On Monday, October 2, 2006, he entered the one-room West Nickel Mines School carrying a 9 mm shotgun. After dismissing all the boys and adults in the school, he barricaded himself in the classroom with the remaining ten female students. The girls ranged in age from six to thirteen. Charles C. Roberts tied up the female students and then shot them one at a time. Five were killed and five wounded. He then killed himself. Roberts was a 32-year-old white male. He was not Amish. His sole connection to the school was that he drove a milk truck in the area.

The community of West Nickel Mines is so small that independent census data is not available. It was, therefore, necessary to look at the township within which West Nickel Mines is located, Bart Township, in Lancaster County, Pennsylvania. The median age for Bart Township was close to the Red Lake neighborhood median population age at 27.7 years old.[21] Also similar to Red Lake was that this was the only other community with fatalities above the trendline and a median household income below the national median. For West Nickel Mines, median household income registered a -$2,951 divergence. This neighborhood had both the largest average household size and the largest average family size of any of the case study neighborhoods. West Nickel Mines had the smallest extent of divergence on the negative side of the national median household income baseline and was closest to the trendline in fatalities. It was just barely above the trendline. Among the outlier cases, it is the only one that did not have double-digit fatalities.

Newtown, Connecticut: Sandy Hook Elementary School

On Friday, December 14, 2012, Adam Lanza, a twenty-year-old white male, began by killing his mother, who had been making straw purchases of guns for him. In the State of Connecticut, Adam Lanza could legally own a long gun or rifle at twenty years old, but not a handgun. At approximately 9:30 a.m., he entered Sandy Hook Elementary School by shooting his way through the glass doors. He entered a first-grade classroom killing the teacher and students. Then he entered the next classroom. Each time he entered a new room, he reloaded his clip even if it wasn't empty. In 5 minutes, he had fired 156 shots, killing 20 children, 6 adults, and himself. Two people were wounded. A jammed 10 mm Glock was found next to his dead body. He had a 9 mm Sig Sauer that was never fired.

Newtown, which is located in Fairfield County, is 11 miles from Danbury, Connecticut, 25 miles from New Haven, Connecticut, and 78 miles from New York City, NY. In other words, it is a suburban jurisdiction with easy access to several major urban centers. The immediate school community was also the most affluent of all the school communities. The median household income for the Sandy Hook school community exceeded the national median by $90,877. It exceeded the median household income for the surrounding city of Newtown by almost $27,000. This community also had the smallest average household size at 2.3 persons.

Parkland, Florida: Marjory Stoneman Douglas High School

On the afternoon of Wednesday, February 14, 2018, Nikolas Cruz, a nineteen-year-old white male, in the prelude to a planned attack, pulled a fire alarm to get students out of the classroom. At approximately 2:21 p.m., he began firing with the AR-15 rifle that he had legally purchased. He was also carrying extra ammunition. In seven minutes, Nikolas Cruz had killed seventeen people and wounded another seventeen, before he slipped out of the school after dropping his weapon and mingling with the exiting students. Subsequently arrested by police, he was charged with seventeen counts of first-degree murder and seventeen counts of attempted first-degree murder.[22] If convicted, he could receive the death penalty. His offer to plead guilty in exchange for a life sentence was rejected by prosecutors.[23] Nikolas Cruz was still awaiting trial at the time this book was written.

The community surrounding the Marjory Stoneman Douglas High School had the second highest positive divergence from the national median at $58,279. The median household income for the neighborhood around the school was $10,000 lower than the median household income for the surrounding city of Parkland. However, the median household income for the school community was still double the median household income for the state of Florida. This neighborhood had the highest percentages for educational attainment among the neighborhoods examined in this section. Ninety-six percent (*n=22,153*) of the population aged twenty-five and over had a high school diploma, and 56% of the population aged twenty-five and over had a bachelor's degree or higher. Sandy Hook's percentages for educational attainment were almost equivalent. These two communities have the greatest extent of divergence from the national median household income. They also had the highest fatality levels among all seventeen school-based mass shooting incidents.

Santa Fe, Texas: Santa Fe High School

At approximately 7:30 a.m. on Friday, May 18, 2018, Dimitrios Pagourtzis, a seventeen-year-old white male, walked into a classroom at Santa Fe High School and started firing. He was carrying a 12-gauge Remington 870 shotgun, and a Rossi .38-caliber snub-nosed revolver both owned by his father.[24] He also had explosives, none of which detonated. Dimitrios Pagourtzis killed eight students and two teachers as well as wounding thirteen before barricading himself into a classroom for a 30-minute standoff with police. Among the wounded was a retired Houston police officer who was serving as a school resource officer. Dimitrios Pagourtziswas charged with capital murder, however, has been found incompetent to stand trial.[25] His trial was delayed while he was sent to a mental health facility for several months.[26] He is believed to have refrained from shooting students he liked, so they could "tell his story."

Among the six communities examined in this section, the immediate neighborhood of Santa Fe High School neighborhood had the lowest positive divergence from the national median at $11,449. The median household income in the Santa Fe High School community was, however, approximately $4,000 higher than the median household income for the surrounding city of Santa Fe. This community had the highest percentage of owner-occupied housing when compared to other cases. Simultaneously, it also had a vacancy percentage more than triple that of the other communities examined in this section. This could be considered an anomaly since it is atypical to see a vacancy rate this high in a community with this level of owner-occupied housing.

CHARACTERISTICS OF PLACE

A multilevel comparison of outlier communities to each other, outlier communities to non-outlier communities, and all school-based mass shooting communities to national socioeconomic conditions will be undertaken in this section. The extent to which the fatality outliers may also be outliers in regards to socioeconomic characteristics will be examined. As will be seen, with a few exceptions, the school communities that were fatality outliers were not very different from the non-outlier school communities.

Community Socioeconomic Comparisons

The six outlier school communities had several commonalities. All incidents involved prior planning. Several involved the planned use of explosives. In each community, the perpetrators had easy availability to the weapons that they used. The question this chapter examines is what, if any, commonalities existed among the different neighborhoods in which these schools existed. In general, the outlier communities were more similar than dissimilar. For instance, all of these communities were racially homogenous. The neighborhoods for Red Lake Senior High School and West Nickel Mines School initially appear as outliers among outliers. In actuality, they are outliers among the entire group of seventeen neighborhoods and jurisdictions that are the subject of this book.

With two exceptions, the seventeen communities for the schools that were the site of these school-based mass shootings had a median age that exceeded the U.S. median.[27] The neighborhoods for Red Lake Senior High School and West Nickel Mines Amish School were both noticeably lower not only from the U.S. median but also from the other school neighborhoods examined in this chapter. While each of the other schools has a median age that is within a four-year range, the median age in the neighborhoods for Red Lake Senior High and West Nickel Mines School is several years younger.

Median age reveals information about the potential stability of a neighborhood. A population with the median age of 36.1 to 40 years old would typically be considered more settled and more prosperous at that age than a community with a median age of 25, as their incomes would also be higher. They would have completed their formal education, be settled in their professional careers, and would have begun starting their families. In addition to the Red Lake and West Nickel Mines school communities, the only other neighborhood with a median age under thirty was the neighborhood surrounding North Park Elementary School in San Bernardino, California.

The communities within which these high-fatality school-based mass shootings occurred are extremely homogenous, and with one exception, that homogeneity was white. Nationally the population is 72.4% white, 12.6% African American, 1.7% American Indian or Alaskan Native, 5.6% Asian, and 7% some other race.[28] Approximately 16% of the population is Hispanic/ Latino. The Majorie Stoneman Douglas High School neighborhood is the only community among the outliers, which comes close to approximating the racial and ethnic diversity of the United States. Because of its location on a closed Indian reservation, Red Lake High School is the only community that is not overwhelmingly white. But, with a population that was 97.6% American Indian, it was still extremely racially homogeneous.

When the examination is expanded to those school communities with low fatalities, three of the remaining eleven school communities had racial or ethnic diversity that exceeded national levels. The communities for Heritage High School (Conyers, Georgia), Success Tech Academy (Cleveland, Ohio), and North Park Elementary School (San Bernardino, California) all had a white population that was below 50%. With the exception of Red Lake, the Success Tech Academy neighborhood was the only community that was a majority-minority neighborhood. It had an African American population of 35.2%, with a white population of 33.1%. That was followed closely by an Asian population of 26.7%, with a 5.8% Hispanic population. Cleveland and San Bernardino are both urban areas. Conyers was a rural area. These three communities also had low or no fatalities resulting from their school-based mass shooting incidents.

Sixty-five percent of the U.S. population over the age of sixteen was in the labor force, with 59.9% employed and 5.1.1% unemployed.[29] The communities for Red Lake Senior High and Sandy Hook Elementary exceeded the national unemployment rate. When examined within the context of their larger economic conditions, however, as discussed earlier, the Sandy Hook community still exceeds median household income at all levels. As a result, their unemployment percentage may not be as detrimental to the community as a whole as it otherwise might be in less advantaged communities.

The outlier communities also tend to be highly educated in comparison to national levels and in comparison to the non-outlier communities. As can be seen from table 4.2, one-half ($n=6$) of the outlier neighborhoods exceeded the national percentage of 27.9% for a bachelor's degree or higher.[30] Only 9% ($n=11$) of non-outlier communities exceeded this level. When it came to the percentage of individuals with a high school diploma or equivalency, 67% ($n=6$) of outlier communities exceeded the national percentage of the 85% of the U.S. population that has a high school diploma or equivalency. For non-outlier communities, every single community placed below the national percentage for high school completion. The school community of Freeman High School (Rockford, Washington) came closest, with 44.5% of its population having a high school diploma or equivalency.

For almost one-third of the population aged twenty-five and over in Nickel Mines, the highest educational attainment was 5th–8th grade. This is reflective of the Amish population in the community for whom 8th grade represents is the end of formal education. The size of the Amish population can also be inferred from the fact that while 99.5% ($n=3,064$) of the population was born in the United States, 44.6% ($n=2,747$) of the population aged five and over spoke an Indo-European language at home. With 31.2% of the population reporting German ancestry, it can be inferred that the language spoken at home was German, which is also consistent for Amish communities.

Linked to education and labor force participation is a community's poverty level. In the United States, 14.6% of the population lives in poverty.[31] In 67% (*n*=6) of these outlier school communities, the percentage of residents living in poverty is less than one-third of the national percentage. There were two exceptions. The percentage of people living in poverty in the community surrounding Red Lake Senior High School was more than double the national percentage of people living in poverty. The Red Lake percentage was ten times the percentage of those living in poverty in the Columbine High School environs. The communities for North Park Elementary School and Success Tech Academy were the only communities other than Red Lake that exceeded the national poverty level at 19.6% and 28%, respectively. However, the poverty levels for their communities were both below the level for the Red Lake school community.

The percentage of persons below the poverty level in the environs of the West Nickel Mines School is just under the national percentage. When it is considered that the highest level of education for almost one-third of the population is the completion of 5th–8th grade, it intuitively feels that the percentage of people living in poverty should be higher than 13%. However, certain factors mitigate against this. Amish populations typically do not educate their children past the eighth grade. But, the end of their formal education does not mean the end of their education in income-generating knowledge and skills. Amish communities are farming communities. Additionally, the Amish are known for their woodwork and craftsmanship. Their furniture products are sold across the country.

The predominant housing type in both the outlier and non-outlier communities is owner-occupied. Excessive housing vacancies can be viewed as a troubling sign in a community. Two years after the 2008 financial meltdown and the home mortgage crisis, the national vacancy rate was 11.4%.[32] Eighty-three percent (*n*=6) of the outlier communities had a housing vacancy percentage ranging from 2.8 to 6%. The predominant vacancy percentage was 6%, which was the percentage in one-half of these communities. The Santa Fe High School community had the highest owner-occupied percentage at 94.7%. It also had the highest percentage of vacancies at 20%, eclipsing the other communities among the outlier group. When compared to the non-outlier communities, the only community that exceeded the housing vacancy rate of Santa Fe community was the Success Tech Academy community, whose Cleveland neighborhood had a housing vacancy rate of 26.2%. This community was the only community where renter-occupied housing exceeded owner-occupied housing.

A shared characteristic among the outlier communities is the predominance of family households. They ranged from a low of 67% in the Columbine community to a high of 85% in the community around Marjory Stoneman

Douglas. Nationwide, family households account for 66% of all households.[33] Family households have declined over the past twenty years, but in the communities examined in this chapter, they remain dominant. Nationally the average household size was 2.58 people, and the average family size was 3.14.[34] The community surrounding West Nickel Mines School has the largest average household size and the largest average family size. There is a strong inverse relationship between the average family size in a community and the number of fatalities from the mass shooting at the school in that community. In other words, fatalities tend to go up as the average family size declines. Small family size is associated with higher-income households, suggesting another connection to relative community affluence and characteristics of school-based mass shootings.

Income Variance and Fatalities

If viewing these seventeen school communities from a regional perspective, as can be seen in table 4.3, the West had the narrowest range for the extent of divergence from the national median with a variance of 29,865. All but one of these neighborhoods were located on the positive side of the baseline. The picture is slightly different when looking at the jurisdiction rather than the school neighborhood. For instance, while the school community for North Park Elementary School had a median household income on the positive side

Table 4.3   School Neighborhoods: Income Variance and Mass Shooting Outcomes

Region	Jurisdiction and Year	Income Variance ($)	Fatalities	Injuries
West	Columbine High School (1999)	22,786	15	21
	Santana High School (2001)	11,596	2	13
	Granite Hills High School (2001)	14,258	0	5
	Marysville Pilchuck High (2014)	12,250	5	1
	Freeman High School (2017)	- 7,079	1	3
	North Park Elementary (2017)	2,660	3	1
Midwest	Red Lake Senior High (2005)	- 21,877	10	7
	Success Tech Academy (2007)	- 21,225	1	4
	Milliard South High School (2011)	14,622	2	2
	Chardon High School (2012)	7,156	3	3
	Madison High School (2016)	- 5,976	0	4
South	Heritage High School (1999)	- 4,907	0	6
	Marshall County High (2018)	- 13,939	2	18
	Marjory Stoneman Douglas (2018)	58,279	17	17
	Santa Fe High School (2018)	11,449	10	13
Northeast	West Nickel Mines School (2006)	-2,951	6	5
	Sandy Hook Elementary (2012)	90,877	28	2

of the baseline, it was located in a jurisdiction, San Bernardino, California, which has a median household income of $20,109 below the baseline. This indicates that while this particular community was barely above the national median household income, when compared to the city in which it was located it was relatively affluent.

The extent of divergence of the median household income of school communities in the Midwest from the national median household income was the second narrowest range in the nation with a variance of 36,499.[35] Sixty percent (*n=5*) of the Midwestern school communities had a median household income that had a negative divergence from the baseline. This region was home to the two communities with the most extreme negative divergence: the neighborhood of Red Lake Senior High School, and the neighborhood of Success Tech Academy. Despite this similarity, these two school neighborhoods looked different when compared to their surrounding jurisdiction. The school community for Red Lake Senior High School, despite the extremity of its negative divergence, had a median household income of just over $1,000 higher than the surrounding jurisdiction of Red Lake. Success Tech Academy's neighborhood, however, was almost $30,000 less than the city of Cleveland within which it was located. The shooting at Red Lake High School had ten fatalities. In comparison, the shooting at Success Tech Academy had one fatality.

The school communities in the South had the second-widest range at 72,218 for the extent of the divergence between their median household income and the national median household income. The two schools in the Southern region placing above the national household median, Marjory Stoneman Douglas High School (Parkland, Florida) and Santa Fe High School (Santa Fe, Texas) averaged 13.5 fatalities. This compares to Heritage High School (Conyer, Georgia) and Marshall County High School (Benton, Kentucky), whose school communities were below the national median household level, and averaged one fatality.

The Northeast region had the largest range for the extent of divergence among its school communities at 93,828. One neighborhood had a positive divergence, and the other a negative divergence from the national median household income baseline. They shared the fact that neither could be considered an urban jurisdiction. Beyond this single point of similarity, the two jurisdictions in the Northeast diverged in ways beyond their median household income. Even though both these school shootings placed above the fatality trendline and were classified as outliers, the median household income for the Sandy Hook Elementary School (Newtown, Connecticut), community was substantially above the national median while West Nickel Mines School (Nickel Mines, Pennsylvania) community was below. Twenty-eight fatalities are associated with Sandy Hook Elementary School and six fatalities for the West Nickel Mines School.

The significance of the neighborhood cannot be understated. While both neighborhood median household income and the median household income for the larger jurisdiction are strongly correlated to the level of fatalities, the neighborhood correlation was slightly stronger than for the jurisdiction as a whole.[36] This suggests that when looking at the relationship between household income (as measured by divergence from the national household median income) and fatalities in a school-based mass shooting, the neighborhood in which the school is located may be more determinative than the larger jurisdiction.

CONCLUSION

For school-based mass shootings, the socioeconomics of place are important. There are distinct differences associated with particular geographic spaces. This chapter focused on identifying some of the differences associated with that space within which school-based mass shootings occur. This chapter focused on addressing the question of "what is" rather than the question of "why it is." The first "what" is that these incidents are more likely to occur in suburban or rural jurisdictions with low population densities, than in urban jurisdictions. Those that do occur in urban areas, or for that matter in suburban or rural jurisdictions with higher population densities, have fewer fatalities.

At least, as important as the jurisdiction, is the community that is the immediate school environs. In regards to the school community, there are certain characteristics that emerge as distinct. For instance, income is strongly correlated to fatalities. Within these suburban and rural jurisdictions, school-based mass shooting communities are further associated with high relative affluence, stable communities with predominately owner-occupied residences, and ease in obtaining weapons. Urban communities or other communities evidencing indicia of poverty, such as high unemployment, lower educational attainment, less community stability, had fewer fatalities.

In identifying these characteristics, the examination of the outlier communities was important. When compared to the national trends, but particularly when compared to the non-outlier communities, an examination of the outlier communities facilitated the identification of distinguishing characteristics. These characteristics are not presented as definitive. They are meant to aid in illustrating the characteristics found in communities and jurisdictions that are the location of school-based mass shootings.

To return to the question of whether these six cases should be considered as outliers, predictors, or even forerunners, the answer is still unknown. A definitive response would, unfortunately, require that more such incidents occur so they could be assessed. What is clear is that these six cases have driven an upward and sustained increase in fatalities over these twenty years. In the absence of interventions at a larger societal level, the two high-fatality incidents occurring three months apart in 2018 may signal the evolution of these cases as predictors and forerunners of what the future may bring.

There is a distinct spatial-temporal footprint left by these high-fatality school-based mass shooting cases. This group of outliers began in the West in Littleton, Colorado (Columbine), then moved to the Midwest to Red Lake, Minnesota (Red Lake Senior High School). The pattern continued eastward with two incidents occurring in the Northeast in West Nickel Mines, Pennsylvania (West Nickel Mines School), and Newtown, Connecticut (Sandy Hook Elementary School). The trajectory turned South to Parklands, Florida (Marjory Stoneman Douglas High School), and then westward, but still in the Southern region to Santa Fe, Texas (Santa Fe High School).

NOTES

1. (DeLeon 2012).
2. (U.S. Bureau of the Census 2017).
3. (U.S. Bureau of the Census 2017).
4. (Ratcliffe et al. 2016).
5. (Ratcliffe et al. 2016).
6. (Pew Research Center 2018).
7. (Pew Research Center 2018).
8. Pearson's $r = -.34$ for population density and Pearson's $r = -.24$ for residential population. Interestingly, this was the reverse when looking at population in relationship to total numbers killed and injured. In that instance, when looking at the relationship with total persons killed and injured, for population density Pearson's $r = -.26$ and for residential population, Pearson's $r = -.34$.
9. Hispanic/Latino is considered an ethnicity as distinct from a racial identity.
10. Unless otherwise indicated the national and state median household income data used in any computations in this chapter were obtained from Table H-8 Median Household Income by State 1984–2018 (U.S. Bureau of the Census 2019). Unless otherwise indicated the median household income and population information for the local jurisdictions was derived from the U.S. Bureau of the Census Quick Facts or the U.S. Census American Community Survey for the particular jurisdiction.
11. The Oklahoma City Bombing was a domestic terrorist attack. A truck bomb was used to blow up the Alfred Pl Murrah Federal Building in Oklahoma City, Oklahoma. Injuries totaled almost 700 and there were 168 deaths.

12. (Margaritoff 2019).

13. (Margaritoff 2019).

14. (Lane and Flowers 2019). Unless otherwise indicated, all descriptive, numerical, and statistical information presented came from that consolidated dataset.

15. (Agnich 2015).

16. (Luzzader 1999).

17. (U.S. Fish and Wildlife Service 2004).

18. (History.Com Editors 2009).

19. (Red Lake Nation 2014).

20. Unless otherwise indicated, the percentages and numbers in this subsection derived from the datasets contained in (U.S. Census Bureau (a) 2000); and (U.S. Census Bureau (b) 2000).

21. Unless otherwise indicated, the percentages and numbers in this section derived from the datasets contained in (U.S. Census Bureau (a) 2000); (U.S. Census Bureau (b) 2000); and (U.S. Census Bureau (a) 2010).

22. (Anderson 2019).

23. (Anderson 2019).

24. (Hanna et al. 2019).

25. (Lozano 2019).

26. (Lozano 2019).

27. (U.S. Census Bureau (a) 2010); and (U.S. Census Bureau 2017).

28. (U.S. Census Bureau (a) 2010).

29. (U.S. Census Bureau (a) 2010).

30. (U.S. Census Bureau (b) 2010).

31. (U.S. Census Bureau 2017).

32. (U.S. Census Bureau (a) 2010).

33. (Lofquist et al. 2012).

34. (U.S. Census Bureau (a) 2010).

35. The range of the divergence is presented as a positive number, rather than a dollar value since the values being compared can be on either side of the baseline.

36. Pearson's *r* for neighborhood was .81 and for jurisdiction it was .75.

Chapter 5

Meeting at the Nexus

School Level and Weapons

INTRODUCTION

This chapter explores the phenomena of school-based mass shootings from the juxtaposition of the grade level of the school and the weapons used at those schools. The search is for identifiable factors connected to the level of the school, whether elementary, middle/junior, or high school, that may have some relationship to the level of fatalities in school-based mass shootings in those schools. Once these factors are identified, can they tell us anything about school-based mass shootings? Underlying these questions is the type and manner of weapons used and whether they vary based on the grade level of the school. This chapter, therefore, examines the seventeen school-based mass shootings from Columbine and Santa Fe using the filter of the grade level of the school that was the site of the mass shooting and the weapons that were used.

These incidents left 105 persons dead and another 125 persons injured.[1] Elementary schools were disproportionately represented among fatalities. Strikingly, while stand-alone middle/junior high schools were the site of almost 20% (n=26) of pre-Columbine mass shootings, there were no mass shootings at comparable schools in the post-Columbine period. There was, however, a mass shooting at a combined junior/senior high school.

The first school-based mass shooting was not found until 1940. It left five people dead and one injured. It was thirty-four years before another school-based mass shooting occurred. Overall there have been forty-three school-based mass shootings; 67% of which have occurred in senior high schools, 21% have occurred in elementary schools, with middle/junior high schools having the lowest at 12%. Since Columbine, 82% (n=17) of the school-based mass shootings have occurred in senior high schools and 18% in elementary schools. None occurred in stand-alone middle/junior high schools. To understand the context, while Columbine and its progeny represent 40% (n=43) of the total number of incidents, they account for 68% of all fatalities.

One question that arises is whether there is some characteristic of elementary school-based mass shootings that makes them different from those occurring in schools at other levels that can account for their disproportionate share of the fatalities. When examined in context, in the past twenty years, two of the three post-Columbine elementary schools that were the site of a mass shooting are found among the top five deadliest school-based mass shootings of all time. This compares to 21% (n=14) of high schools that are found among the top five deadliest school-based mass shootings of all time. Elementary schools are further distinguished by the fact that unlike the senior high schools, in each of their mass shooting incidents, the number of fatalities exceeded the number of injured. This is also a complete reversal from elementary school shootings pre-Columbine. This chapter looks at the grade level of the school and weapons used in the shooting for an insight into changes in fatality levels. As part of this examination, it is necessary to also incorporate selected perpetrator aspects for consideration.

Weapons from a sample of incidents are described. They do not include the weapons used in all incidents. But for those that are described, the descriptions are detailed, and many could be considered excessive. That is deliberate. These are the weapons that are being brought into the nation's schools. Some of these are essentially weapons of war. Individual familiarity with weapons varies. An underlying goal of this chapter is to provide, for the unfamiliar, a sense of the weapons that confront our children, their teachers, and school administrators when school-based mass shootings occur. To illustrate what, in some instances, might be the last thing these victims see.

ELEMENTARY SCHOOLS

Understanding the connection between school level and weapons at the elementary school level can best be done when viewing these post-Columbine elementary schools in comparison to their pre-Columbine counterparts. When examining the differences between elementary school mass shootings pre- and post-Columbine, several major distinctions emerge, the fatality: injury ratio, perpetrator demographics, and weapons used. It is particularly the latter two distinctions that contribute to the exceptionally high fatality count among the elementary schools that have been the site of mass shootings during the twenty-year period that is the subject of this book. They will be discussed in this section following an overview of mass shootings as they occur at elementary schools. The most significant change occurring at elementary school mass shootings post-Columbine was twofold. First, the aggregated fatality count was significantly higher. Second, in each instance, the number of fatalities always exceeded the number of injuries.

The most recent twenty years looks very different for elementary school mass shootings than earlier years. The very first mass shooting at an elementary school occurred on January 17, 1974, at the Clara W. Barton Elementary School in Chicago, Illinois. This was thirty years after the first school-based mass shooting and was only the second school-based mass shooting. The shooting at Clara Barton Elementary School has two primary distinctions. It was one of only two elementary school shootings where the perpetrator was a juvenile, and it is the only elementary school shooting where none of the victims were students. The son of a police officer, Steven Guy, age fourteen, was angry over being transferred from the school to the social adjustment center. He took his father's .45-caliber pistol and .38-caliber pistol then went to the school where he killed the principal. The assistant principal and a security guard were wounded when they confronted him. Steven Guy later headed to the classroom of his former teacher and grazed the teacher's arm.

The shooting at Clara Barton Elementary School set the trend in regards to fatalities for the elementary school mass shootings that followed. Eighty-six percent (n=7) of the pre-Columbine elementary school shootings had only one or two fatalities. With a few exceptions, the weapons used were handguns. The only female juvenile, among all school-based mass shooters, Brenda Spencer, used a .22-caliber air pellet rifle fitted with a telescope as she fired from her front porch across the street toward the Cleveland Elementary School in San Diego, California (January 29, 1979). Patrick Edward Purdy used the only known pre-Columbine assault weapon at the Stockton Schoolyard—Cleveland Elementary School in Stockton, California (January 17, 1989). Davis and Doris Young used a gasoline bomb along with a handgun at Cokeville Elementary School in Cokeville, Wyoming (May 18, 1986).

Elementary schools in the post-Columbine environment, have had a disproportionate number of the fatalities resulting from school-based mass shootings when compared to those occurring at schools of other levels. Elementary schools were the site of three of the seventeen post-Columbine school-based mass shootings. They represented 17% of the total number of all school-based mass shootings during this period. However, mass shootings at elementary schools accounted for 35% of all fatalities, and only 6% of injuries. These three shootings were responsible for a total of thirty-seven fatalities and eight injuries.

During the twenty-year period covered by this book, several noticeable changes occurred in mass shootings at the elementary school level. None are more visible than the relationship between fatalities and injuries. In every single elementary school mass shooting before Columbine, the number of injuries always exceeded the number of fatalities. In the ones occurring after Columbine, that is reversed with the number of fatalities in each incident being higher. It is a post-Columbine elementary school that ranks as the deadliest school-based mass shooting to date. The mass shootings at these three elementary schools averaged 12 fatalities and 2.6 injuries per incident. These three incidents alone produced a total number of forty-five individuals killed or wounded.

This aggregated total of 37 persons killed and eight persons injured at three elementary schools post-Columbine compares to 16 fatalities and 144 injured in seven pre-Columbine elementary schools. The extraordinarily high injury count for the pre-Columbine incidents is traceable to two schools. Cokeville Elementary School in Cokeville, Wyoming, was the site of a hostage-taking resulting in two deaths and seventy-four injuries in 1986. This large number of injuries occurred when the bombs strapped to one of the hostage-takers exploded. There were two deaths from firearms, the husband and wife per-petrators. The second incident was the Stockton Schoolyard-Cleveland Elementary School shooting. It is the only pre-Columbine school-based mass shooting at an elementary school known to involve an assault weapon. Patrick Edward Purdy using an AK-47 assault rifle killed five children and wounded another thirty-two students and teachers before killing himself. Even if these two schools are excluded, the resulting eight fatalities and thirty-eight injuries from the remaining five schools are still consistent with the pre-Columbine elementary school pattern of injuries exceeding fatalities.

Perpetrators

Elementary perpetrators have changed over time. They have become older and more monolithic. The elementary school mass shooter of the previous twenty years was typically white, with a prior or existing connection to the targeted school. He was also male, with an average age of thirty-five years old. The disaggregated picture of these three incidents is more varied. The perpetrators ranged in age from twenty to fifty-three. Two of the perpetra-tors had a prior or existing connection to their targeted school. The youngest was a former student, while the oldest was the estranged spouse of a teacher. The one black perpetrator in this group was also the only black perpetrator among the eighteen school-based mass shooters at all grade levels during the twenty-year period that is the focus of this book.[2] The remaining elementary school perpetrators were white. The one shared commonality was that each committed suicide at the end of their attack.

This perpetrator type averaged a decade older than their pre-Columbine counterpart, who had an average age of twenty-five with an age range from fourteen to forty-five. One-half (n=8) of the pre-Columbine perpetrators of elementary school shootings had a prior or existing connection to the target school.[3] Three were former students, and as to the fourth, the school was built on the site of his childhood home. Pre-Columbine elementary school perpetrators included: four white males, one black male, and three white female perpetrators. The only female perpetrators pre-Columbine, for any school-based mass shooting, were at the elementary school level. Post-Columbine, there were no female perpetrators at any grade level. Two juveniles are included in this group of pre-Columbine elementary school mass shooting perpetrators, a fourteen-year-old male and a sixteen-year-old female. Sixty-three percent (n=8) of the pre-Columbine perpetrators committed suicide or died during the incident. The other three were convicted and sent to prison. In comparison, 100% of the post-Columbine perpetrators of elementary school-based mass shootings committed suicide.

Weapons

A variety of weapons were used in these three shootings. A 9mm handgun was used at West Nickel Mines School in Nickel Mines, Pennsylvania (October 2, 2006).[4] West Nickel Mines School was the first post-Columbine mass shooting at an elementary school. Charles C. Roberts killed five and wounded another five female students before killing himself. After separating the female students from the teacher and the male students, he proceeded to execute the girls after tying them up.[5] Twelve years later, a .357 magnum revolver was used at the North Park Elementary School mass shooting in San Bernardino, California (April 10, 2017), producing a total of three fatalities with one person injured. Cedric Anderson killed his estranged wife, who was a special education teacher at the school. He also killed one student, wounded another student, before killing himself. The North Park Elementary school shooting can be also be described as a domestic shooting with collateral damage. This shooting is notable in that it is the only elementary school shooting post-Columbine that did not involve a semiautomatic weapon.

The picture was different at Sandy Hook Elementary School in Newtown, Connecticut (December 14, 2012), with its associated total of thirty fatalities[6] and injuries. The one perpetrator had multiple semiautomatic weapons, including an Izhmash Saiga 12 gauge semiautomatic shotgun, which is similar to the AK assault rifle.[7] It is manufactured by Izhmash Russian State Arms Company and weighs up to a maximum of 7.93 lbs, with a maximum length of 45.07 inches. It has a barrel that can stretch up to 22.83 inches in length, with a magazine capacity of up to 8 rounds standard. An unidentified model of the Glock 20, 10mm semiautomatic handgun with a magazine capacity of 15 rounds was also present at the Sandy Hook shooting. There was a Sig Sauer P226 9mm semiautomatic handgun that weighed 34.4oz and was 7.7

inches in length. It had a barrel length of 4.4 inches, a width of 1.5 inches, and a magazine capacity of up to 10 rounds standard.[8] Also present was a Bushmaster XM-15 .223-caliber semiautomatic rifle[9] similar to the military grade M-16 or Armalite Rifle (AR-15) weighing 7lbs, 16 inches in length, with a magazine capacity of 30 rounds standard with an adjustable rear sight.

It is this incident, which has the unfortunate distinction of having the highest fatality count of all K–12 school-based mass shootings in the United States. With this amount of firepower carried by one person, it is easy to understand how the twenty-eight fatalities at Sandy Hook Elementary School in 2012 were almost double to that of the fifteen fatalities at Columbine that so stunned the nation in 1999. It was the Sandy Hook shooting that led to the lawsuit against Remington Arms, alleging violation of CUTPA discussed in chapter 2. In looking at post-Columbine elementary schools, there are a couple of factors that stand out. The first is that none of the perpetrators were current students at the target school. In other words, these shootings were not committed by elementary school students. Each one was committed by some-one who came into the school, specifically to do harm. The second factor is that there is a clear connection between the lethality of the weapons brought into the schools and the level of fatalities.

HIGH SCHOOLS

Mass shootings at high schools are more nuanced than those occurring at other levels. The prime differences are the perpetrator's affiliation with the school, the age of the perpetrator, and how the weapons have been acquired by the perpetrator. Since Columbine, mass shootings at high schools have continued in the pattern of injuries exceeding fatalities, although there have been changes in how this pattern manifests.

Fourteen of the seventeen post-Columbine school-based mass shootings occurred at high schools. They resulted in 68 fatalities and 117 injuries. While the mass shooting incidents occurring at high schools in the past twenty years have some similarities with those occurring at elementary schools, there are more differences. Unlike the mass shootings at elementary schools, which had several noticeable changes over time, the changes in mass shootings at high schools during this twenty-year period were subtle in their manifestation. As distinct from the post-Columbine elementary school pattern, where fatalities always exceeded injuries, at the high school level, injuries continued to exceed fatalities for 64% (n=14) of the post-Columbine incidents. This does represent a decline from the pre-Columbine era, where injuries exceeded fatalities in 97% (n=14) of high school mass shootings incidents. What this means is that overall while injuries continue to exceed fatalities for post-Columbine high school mass shootings, there are increased numbers of incidents where fatalities exceed injuries.

During this twenty-year period, high school mass shootings averaged 4.85 fatalities and 8.35 injuries or a fatality to injury ratio of approximately 1:2. This compares to the post-Columbine elementary school fatality to injury ratio of approximately 5:1. This fatality-injury relationship is a key area of difference between mass shootings occurring at high schools and those occurring at elementary schools. Other areas of comparison are selected perpetrator demographics and weapons used. A total of 185 individuals were killed or wounded in high school mass shootings since Columbine. It is the juxtaposition of weapons with perpetrators that is the most jarring in examining these incidents.

Perpetrators

As with elementary school mass shooters, a majority (85%) of the fifteen high school mass shooters during the past twenty years were white.[10] Thirteen percent (n=15) were American Indian. None of this group of perpetrators was black. None were female. Unlike the perpetrators in elementary school mass shootings, none of whom were current students, 80% (n=15) of these perpetrators were enrolled at the high school when the incident occurred, the remaining 20% were former students of the targeted school. The perpetrators were all male, with an average age of 16.2 years, one-half the average age of the elementary school perpetrators. With an age range of fourteen to nineteen, the oldest perpetrator from a high school mass shooting was younger than the youngest perpetrator from an elementary school mass shooting. It should be noted that while a substantial increase had occurred in the average age among perpetrators of elementary school mass shootings over their pre-Columbine average age, there was no such difference among the high school perpetrators. One-third (n=15) of the high school perpetrators post-Columbine committed suicide at the end as compared to 7% (n=14) of their pre-Columbine counterparts.

Weapons

Semiautomatic weapons were involved in 57% (n=14) of high school mass shooting incidents. As may be expected, they produced a disproportionate share of fatalities. The incidents in which semiautomatic weapons were used accounted for 82% (n=68) of the fatalities and 61% (n=117) of the injuries from post-Columbine mass shootings at high schools. This was a fatality level that was almost 50% higher than incidents that did not involve semiautomatic weapons. The mass shootings that involved semiautomatic weapons also appear to have a pattern of multiple weapon involvement. A single high school mass shooting involved the Intratec TEC-DC9 9mm semiautomatic pistol manufactured by Intratec Firearms, Inc. weighing 55 oz and 12.48 inches in length. It has a 5 inch barrel able to carry a 10 to 72 round magazine with a muzzle velocity of 1,200 to 1,400 feet per second and a range of 50 to 100 yards.[11] This incident also involved the Hi-Point 995 9mm carbine rifle manufactured by Hi-Point Firearms weighing 6.25lbs. It is 31 inches in length with a 16.5 inch barrel able to carry from a 10 to 15 round magazine with adjustable sights with a velocity of 1,400 feet per second and a range of 100–200 yards.[12] The incident further involved a 9mm semiautomatic handgun. These weapons were used by a seventeen and eighteen year old in the Columbine High School shooting in Littleton, Colorado (April 20, 1999) to kill thirteen and injure twenty-one before killing themselves.

The Ruger Mark II .22-caliber semiautomatic pistol manufactured by Strum, Ruger & Company, Inc., a rim fire pistol that is magazine fed with a capacity of 9 to 10 shots with an adjustable rear sight;[13] and the .40-caliber Glock 23 semiautomatic pistol manufactured by Smith & Wesson weighing 21.16 oz, 6.85 inches in length, 5 inches in height with a barrel length of 4.03 inches, 1.18 inches in width using a 10 to 13 round magazine[14] were used in the Red Lake Senior High School shooting in Red Lake, Minnesota (March 21, 2005) by a 16-year-old who killed 9 and wounded 7 before killing himself.

A .40-caliber semiautomatic, with no readily available manufacturer information, was used in the Millard South High School Shooting in Omaha, Nebraska, by an eighteen year old who killed one and wounded two before killing himself. The .40-caliber Beretta Px4 Storm weighing 27.7 oz has a length between 7.55 inches, with a barrel length of 4 inches; it is 1.42 inches in width, has a height of 5.51 inches and sight radius of 5.75 inches with a 14 round magazine capacity.[15] It was used by a fifteen year old in the Marysville Pilchuck High School shooting in Marysville, Washington, (October 24, 2014) to kill four people and injure one before killing himself.

The Ruger Mark III a .22-caliber semiautomatic handgun manufactured by Strum, Ruger & Company Inc., a rim fire pistol that is magazine fed with a capacity of ten shots[16] was used by a seventeen year old in the Chardon High School shooting in Chardon, Ohio (February 27, 2012) to kill three and injure three others. The Sig Sauer P238, a .38-caliber semiautomatic handgun weighs 15.2 oz, is 5.5 inches in length with a 2.7-inch barrel, 1.1 inches in width, 3.9 to 4.3 inches in height depending on the model, with a 9 to 18 round magazine capacity. It was used by a fourteen year old in the Madison High School Shooting in Middletown, Ohio (February 29, 2016), where four persons were injured, with no fatalities. An AR-style weapon similar to the Colt Armalite Rifle (AR-15) with an adjustable sight, 31.5 to 35 inches in length with a 16.1 inch barrel, weighing 6.3lbs with a 33 round magazine capacity[17] was used by a fifteen year old in the Freeman High School shooting in Rockford, Washington (September 13, 2017) to kill one and injure three. It was also used by a nineteen year old in the Marjory Stoneman Douglas High School Shooting in Parkland, Florida (February 14, 2018), where seventeen were killed and another seventeen persons injured.

All the semiautomatic weapons have an automatic ejecting feature with a quick reload. Any weapon that shoots more than one shot or can be modified to shoot more than one shot without manually reloading by a single function of the trigger is considered a machine gun.[18] What is most noticeable about the weapons used in the high school mass shootings is the weight or relative lack thereof. While the heaviest weapons weighed up to 8 pounds, most appeared to weigh between 2 and 4 pounds. Some barely hit 1 pound in weight. Many of these weapons weigh less than a laptop or a heavy textbook. This section only described the weapons used in some of the high school mass shootings to give a general sense of the types of semiautomatic weapons being used. It is not intended to suggest that these are the only high school mass shootings that involved semiautomatic weapons. There were five, post-Columbine high school incidents that did not involve semiautomatic weapons, and of those incidents, 80% (n=5) involved a .22-caliber revolver. The 35% (n=14) of incidents that did not involve semiautomatic weapons were responsible for 15% (n=68) of all fatalities and 38% (n=117) of all injuries. This suggests that those high school mass shootings that involved the use of semiautomatic weapons were responsible for the increases in fatalities at the high school level.

CONCLUSIONS

This chapter began with a summary discussion of mass shootings at the different grade levels. It then looked at the fatalities/injuries at these different school levels as well as characteristics associated with the perpetrators and weapons used for the period stretching from Columbine through Santa Fe to examine whether there was an identifiable pattern between fatalities and injuries, these characteristics, and the school level. When taking a composite overview look, ten of the forty-three school-based mass shootings identified as occurring in the period between 1919 and 2018 occurred in elementary schools. Five occurred in middle/junior high schools, and twenty-eight occurred in senior high schools. These incidents have presented differently at the different school levels. This chapter does not attempt to explore the reasons for the absence of stand-alone middle/junior high schools as mass shooting sites post-Columbine.

Mass shootings at elementary schools are very different from those occurring in schools at other levels. Two principle differences are the number of fatalities and the age of the perpetrator. Since Columbine, mass shootings at elementary schools have had a disproportionate number of fatalities when compared to their percentage of overall incidents. The three shootings occurring at elementary schools during the twenty-year period, which is the subject of this book, account for 35% (n=105) of all school-based mass shooting fatalities during this period. Yet, elementary schools only accounted for 18% (n=17) of the number of incidents. It is an elementary school that has the unfortunate distinction of being the site of the deadliest K–12 school-based mass shooting. In the overall total of school-based mass shootings, the fatalities incurred at Sandy Hook fit into an emerging and disturbing trend. In regards to mass shootings among all elementary schools, pre-, and post-Columbine, where 60% (n=10) of incidents have no more than two fatalities, they are an outlier.

All post-Columbine elementary school-based mass shootings concluded in suicide. Thirty-six percent (n=14) of all post-Columbine high school-based mass shootings concluded in suicide, 50% resulted in convictions of the perpetrator, with 14% whose judicial proceedings were still ongoing at the time this book was written. While the dubious distinction of perpetrator belongs to white males (84%) in these seventeen incidents, the more telling connections between perpetrators and schools are related to student status and age. Eighty-nine percent (n=18) of all perpetrators were current or former students. While 78% (n=18) were eighteen or younger, 61% (n=18) were under the age of eighteen. The differences in student status in regards to the two school levels in this chapter are important. None (n=3) of the elementary school shooters were current students. Eighty percent (n=14) of the high school shooters were current students. At the high school level, this means that these are not individuals coming in from outside the school to commit these acts. In most instances, they are already there. This has implications for how schools approach security. More disturbing, however, is the lethality and sheer magnitude of the weapons that were readily obtainable for individuals who, in the overwhelming number of cases, were juveniles.

Fifty-two percent of weapons used by perpetrators, in post-Columbine school-based mass shootings, were taken from the home of a parent. They were usually owned by the father or in the father's possession, or owned by a legal guardian. Twenty-four percent of all weapons used were purchased by the perpetrator or friend, while 18% were taken from grandparents, great-grandparents, or other family members. For example, as many as two weapons were obtained per house in the shootings at Heritage High School in Conyers, Georgia (May 20, 1999), Granite Hills High School in El

Cajon, California (March 22, 2001), and Santa Fe High School in Santa Fe, Texas (May 18, 2018). The source of 6% of weapons acquisition remains unknown.

Sandy Hook Elementary School in Newton, Connecticut, was the only elementary school where a perpetrator was legally unable to purchase the guns they used and hence had acquired the weapons used in the shooting from the home of a parent or legal guardian. The other post-Columbine elementary school shooters were old enough to legally make their gun purchases. Adam Lanza's mother was an avid gun collector. In addition to making legal purchases for herself, she also made straw purchases for her son, who at twenty was too young to buy these particular weapons. It is unclear which of the weapons used were taken from the mother's personal collection and which were among the straw purchases made for Adam Lanza.

The simple reason for the fact that the majority of the elementary school perpetrators procured their own weapons while the high school perpetrators take them from their home, usually from their parents, is based on the age of the perpetrators. All of the post-Columbine high school perpetrators were younger than the post-Columbine elementary school perpetrators. With few exceptions, they were not even old enough to purchase long guns, which can be purchased at the age of eighteen in many states. Nikolas Cruz was able to purchase the weapons he used at Parkland, even though he was legally unable to purchase a handgun because he was under the age of twenty-one.

NOTES

1. (Lane Pixley and Flowers 2019). Unless otherwise indicated, all numerical and statistical data presented is based on that dataset.

2. There were two perpetrators at Columbine High School, making of total of eighteen perpetrators for the seventeen incidents.

3. Cokeville Elementary School involved two perpetrators, for a total of eight perpetrators for the seven incidents.

4. West Nickel Mines School in Nickel Mines Pennsylvania was an Amish School. Amish schools are typically one room schoolhouses going up to eighth grade. Therefore, this school was included with the elementary schools.

5. (LancasterPa.com n.d.).

6. This number includes, Adam Lanza, the perpetrator, and his mother whom he shot before heading to the school.

7. (Popenker n.d.).

8. The Sig Sauer P226 9mm semiautomatic handgun found at the scene was believed to have been unused however.

9. (Bushmaster Firearms 2006).

10. There have been fourteen instances of mass shootings, since Columbine, at high schools. The two perpetrators at Columbine make a total of fifteen individuals who perpetrated mass shootings at high schools.

11. (Intratec Firearms n.d.).

12. (Hi-Point Firearms n.d.).

13. (Ruger (a) n.d.).

14. (GlockStore.com n.d.).

15. (Beretta.com n.d.).

16. (Ruger (b) n.d.).

17. (Colt n.d.).

18. 27 CFR, Part B, § 479.11.

Chapter 6

School-Based Mass Shooters

INTRODUCTION

Efforts have understandably focused on the issue of how to identify potential school shooters as if there are identifiable predictive factors. The default position among the public when mass shootings occur is to focus on mental illness. To some extent, this is driven by news media framing in the wake of mass shootings.[1] It is driven by public policy, in which each time a mass shooting occurs, the response is to discuss additional restrictions on the ability of the mentally ill to obtain firearms. The examination of these shootings within a social or cultural context has lagged behind.[2] Metzl et al. argued that the relationship between individual mental illness and gun violence was less causal than popularly assumed and that gun violence needed to be viewed in the social context in which it occurred.[3] They identified the role played by race in shifting the framework for mass shooters to mental illness, further arguing that shifting the focus in mass shootings to mental illness served to shift the focus away from guns.[4] This was more explicitly discussed by Mingus et al. who described the role of white privilege in the designation of mental illness as the causative factor for mass shooters.[5]

This is not to negate the role played by psychological factors in school-based mass shootings. But it is essential to focus on the correct issue. Skeem et al. pointed to research identifying a weak relationship between serious mental illness and mass shootings, but expressly disclaimed its role as a causal factor or explanatory factor in mass violence. They enunciated the importance of distinguishing between severe mental illness and emotional distress when examining mass shootings.[6] As an illustration, Skeem et al. used the example of schizophrenia for severe mental illness in comparison to an employee distraught for being fired as an example of emotional distress.[7]

Focusing preventive strategies on the removal of firearms from those with diagnosed mental illnesses will have no impact on stopping the distraught employee.[8] The disadvantage of relying on psychological factors as the exclusive or even primary lens through which these incidents are viewed is that it facilitates overlooking or avoiding factors that might otherwise be considered as warning signs.

This is similar to the conclusion of Blum et al. who found that placing the focus exclusively on a shooter's psychological factors neglects the broader contributing social context or influence. As an alternative to an exclusively psychological approach, some researchers have used General Strain Theory from the field of Criminology, as a possible explanation. A central tenet of General Strain Theory is the role played by negative emotions in mediating the association between strain and deviant behavior.[9] Utilizing three mass shootings, Blum et al. examined the violence of the mass shooter as a response to strain, specifically unpleasant life experiences. The prevalence of social isolation or lack of community integration among the shooters was also found to be a common factor.[10] Aseltine et al. posited that anger functioned to mediate the impact between strain as related to negative life events and conflict with family members and adolescent deviance. This anger then manifests in aggression or violent acts.[11]

A study of seventy-three public mass shootings in the U.S. between 1983 and 2013 conducted by Lemieux found that 56% of perpetrators had exhibited signs of mental illness before the shooting incident.[12] However, this study also found that perpetrators who had preexisting signs of mental illness were no more destructive in terms of the number of victims, weapons, or a concluding suicide attempt by the perpetrator than those who did not exhibit signs of mental illness before the shooting incident.[13] Mental illness and bullying have dominated when the focus is narrowed to mass shootings occurring in schools. Much of the research in this area has a qualitative microlevel focus on the perpetrator as society attempts to ascertain explanations for their actions. Langman looked at two school shootings, in conjunction with other youthful violent offenses, to examine the issue of why young people become violent and to look for the identification of warning signs.[14] Later, he looked at perpetrator motivations in forty-eight national and international cases to facilitate recognition of potential perpetrators and identify prevention needs.[15]

Rice et al. hypothesized that adolescent mass shootings resulted from thwarted progress along the normal developmental spectrum. Specifically, they focused on a young male's failure to effectuate the normal separation from their maternal figure (i.e., mother, grandmother, etc.) as a risk factor.[16] Using Adam Lanza, the Sandy Hook shooter, Rice et al. pointed to the distant relationship Adam Lanza had with his father and posited that the type of mother-son relationship he experienced, enmeshed in violence and an inability to separate is a factor for future mass violence.[17] During part of the time, Adam Lanza lived in his mother's basement; he would only communicate with her by email. However, she continued to encourage him in their shared gun hobby by making straw purchases of firearms for him.[18] Rice et al. found that for this particular type of shooter, matricide frequently precedes the mass killing, despite the fact that matricide is relatively rare.

Newman et al. took a slightly different approach in their study of school shooters. While also geared toward the identification of perpetrator warning signs (similar to the psychological perspectives), Newman et al. used two school shootings as the basis for a sociological study of the role of schools and communities in regards to the unmet needs of troubled youth.[19] Lenhardt et al. narrowed the focus to the extent to which schools had control over causal factors. In a study of fifteen school shootings involving a known target, either a classmate, teacher, or school building, Lenhardt et al. found that the underlying cause for what is known as targeted school shooters was the interaction of complex variables in the life of the shooter rather than a single cause.

This interaction involved variables such as personality, family dynamics, as well as environmental or contextual factors.[20] Only the environmental or contextual factors were found to be within the control of the school. An example of the interplay of these factors would be when a student with poor coping skills (personality factor) is rejected or isolated by their peers (environmental factor), violence can result.[21] This compares with Welton et al. who, in their study of rampage school shooters, found that while the majority had experienced bullying and been ostracized by their peers prior to the incident, they also noted other types of chronic and acute strain in their lives.[22] Some studies of school shootings involve rampage shootings as distinct from mass shootings. However, they can overlap. The definition of rampage shootings is broader than that of mass shootings since rampage shootings can involve as few as two victims as compared to four for a mass shooting. As with mass shootings, rampage shootings often have variation in their definition.

In their study, Welton et at. defined rampage shooting as those that (1) are intended to kill more than one individual in a specific location, (2) may or may not involve specifically targeted victims, and (3) the location is a symbol or is associated with negative emotion. This is similar to Fox et al. who envisioned rampage shootings as directed against the institution, that is, the school, rather than an individual. They defined rampage shootings, for their research, as having the following characteristics: (1) they occur at school or at a school event; (2) the shooter is a current or former student; (3) there are multiple victims or targets; and (4) at least some victims were either symbolically or randomly targeted.[23]

Fox et al. took an institutional perspective on the role of schools in school shootings. They theorized that rampage school shootings could be viewed as instances of organizational deviance on the part of the school, in which the failure to prevent school shootings is the normal outcome of a school's routine organizational processes and activities.[24] The normal institutional or organizational process identified by Fox et al. is *information loss* such that, in most instances, school officials are unaware prior to the shooting that the shooter was experiencing difficulties such as severe emotional or mental trauma or that they had such high levels of rage against the school.[25] There are four reasons identified for this information loss. First is the absence of resources directed toward staff and faculty training in identifying and addressing students' emotional and social needs. The second reason is that those resources that do exist in this area go toward those students whose behavior overtly disrupts the school's operations and overlooks those with minor infractions. The third reason is that existing student information is fragmented across different operational levels. Finally, the information that does exist can be missed due to cultural notions and common cognitive practices.[26]

The difficulty is that the traits and characteristics often identified are also found in the larger number of students who are not involved in school shootings.[27] This is one of the reasons why there is no profile of a school-based mass shooter. However, school-based mass shooters can be studied in a manner that leads to the development of typologies or models. A typology is simply a method for heuristic identification and arrangement of items into categories. Typologies, however, present an ability to examine shared characteristics and commonalities. Similarly, model development presents a framework for analyzing the perpetrators. More importantly, typologies and models can suggest intervention and response strategies. Instead of focusing exclusively on the individual perpetrator's psychological traits, this chapter aims to expand the frame of reference by examining their behavior within a broader social context.

Some of the studies described in this chapter specifically looked at school-based mass shooters. The majority looked at perpetrators from a wider range of categories, such as school-based rampage shooters, public mass shooters, or active shooters. Following a discussion of several models and typologies, this chapter will look at individual characteristics of the eighteen perpetrators of the seventeen school-based mass shooting incidents in the twenty-year period being studied.

SELECTED MODELS AND TYPOLOGIES

This section looks at four approaches to understanding school shooters. The first two approaches, "A Model for Differentiating School Shooter Characteristics" by Ioannou et al. and the "Adolescent Insider Masculinity

(AIM) Model by Farr, utilize a psychologically based classification system. The last two approaches bring different perspectives to the incorporation of factors beyond a perpetrator's mental health into the causality calculus. They are the "Assessment-Intervention Model" by FBI-NCAVC, and the "Initial Involvement Classification Typology" by Osborne et al.

A Model for Differentiating School Shooter Characteristics, Ioannou et al.

Ioannou et al. evaluated forty school shootings to develop a model to differentiate school shooter characteristics. Their analysis of the co-occurrence of eighteen characteristics or risk factors resulted in the identification of three distinct themes: Disturbed School Shooter, Rejected School Shooter, and Criminal School Shooter.[28] The Disturbed School Shooter theme included nine of the risk factors: on medication for a mental health issue; a previously diagnosed mental illness; played violent video games or watched violent films; was bullied at school; male; had suicidal thoughts; violent writings or drawings; was a loner, and kept a journal. The Rejected School Shooter included four of the risk factors: relationship breakup leading to identified feelings of rejection, past suicide attempt, abused at home, and suspension or expulsion from school. The Criminal School Shooter is characterized by five variables: a fascination with weapons, past criminal convictions; past violent behavior; violent behavior against family members; and multiple offenders involved in planning, or implementing the offense. The Disturbed School Shooter was the theme most frequently occurring. It was the dominant theme identified among school shooters at 60%, followed by the Rejected School Shooter at 12.5%, with the Criminal School Shooter theme identified least often at 7.5%.[29]

Adolescent Insider Masculinity (AIM) Model, Farr

Farr focused on the role of failing masculinity as a cause of rampage school shootings developing a model entitled Adolescent Insider Masculinity (AIM). It is a model that is equally as viable for school-based mass shootings. This model identifies four defining characteristics by which adolescent males are traditionally judged by their peers. These characteristics are summarized as: being cool, proving heterosexuality, repudiating femininity, and being tough.[30] In a study of thirty-one shooters from twenty-nine rampage school shootings between 1995 and 2005, Farr essentially found a vicious cycle—the shooters failed in some aspect of the AIM model, they were made aware of these failings by peers, and they responded with hyper-demonstrations of AIM norms particularly violence. Within the AIM model, Farr identified subgroupings of personal problems that impacted the outcomes.

The three subgroupings were: Psychiatric Disorder, Family Turbulence, and Situational Volatility. The largest number of people were killed by those who fell within the Psychiatric Disorder subgroup.[31] They were followed by those in the Family Turbulence subgroup, with the lowest number killed by those within the Situational Volatility subgroup.[32] The theme of failing masculinity has been a recurring theme in explanations for school shootings.

Assessment-Intervention Model, FBI-NCAVC

An Assessment-Intervention Model was developed by the Federal Bureau of Investigation's (FBI) National Center for the Analysis of Violent Crime (NCAVC). The NCAVC sought to provide a framework for assessing a student to determine if they have the motivation, means, and intent to carry out a threat. The uniqueness is the inclusion of an intervention component as part of the model. This Model advocates an inclusive assessment of the student in four major areas, comprising the Four-Pronged Assessment Model: (1) student personality, (2) family dynamics, (3) school dynamics, and the student's role in those dynamics, and (4) social dynamics.[33] Depending on the classification level assigned to the threat (low, medium, high) and the outcomes of the four-pronged assessment, interventions ranged from school-based involvement to law enforcement involvement.[34] Equally as important, the NCAVC report spoke to the need for further study on a range of issues as well as training for school personnel on threat assessment.

Significantly, the NCAVC report also addressed the need to educate students about "leakage," which is defined as the inadvertent or unintentional disclosure by the student of an impending violent act.[35] Post-incident reviews have revealed that many shooters have "leaked" or "signaled" their intent to their classmates in ways that were only fully recognized in hindsight. Leakage is a common phenomenon in these incidents. Lenhardt et al. found that while only 13% of the secondary school shooters they examined had informed parents or another adult, 87% had informed peers of their intentions, sometimes with extremely detailed advanced information. In their study, none of those peers reported the planned assault to school officials. They also found that 53% of the shooters described their intentions in writing or on other types of school assignments offering an additional opportunity for a third-party to become aware of the intentions.[36]

Initial Involvement Classification Typology, Osborne et al.

Osborne et al. studied active shooters through the application of rational choice perspective and crime script analysis. They found that motivation served as the organizing theme for active shooter event occurrence, identifying three categories of events: autogenic, victim-specific, and ideological. These initial involvement classifications were used to examine: offender characteristics, event characteristics (including both planning and implementation), and event conclusion. Autogenic active shooter events constituted 24.6% of the studied cases.[37] They were typically considered to lack a specific motive since, typically, there was no relationship between the shooter and the victims. In short, autogenic events are characterized by a "self-generated" conflict where victims are proxies, and revenge is against an abstract issue. Autogenic shooter events were also characterized by having the highest percentage of instances of confirmed or suggested mental illness in the offender.[38]

Victim-specific active shooter events were the most common of the studied cases at 63.4%.[39] These events are characterized as seeking revenge against specific individuals and typically include a clearly identifiable precipitating event.[40] Ideologically active shooter events constituted 11.3% of the studied cases and were the least common.[41] Beyond the characteristic of an underlying ideological basis, they had similar characteristics to the autogenic shooter events: victims as proxies, and revenge as an abstraction.[42] Osborne et al. used active shooters as the subject of their study. The question that arises is the extent to which their initial involvement classifications can be applied to the subject of mass shooters who are school-based.

PERPETRATOR DESCRIPTIONS

This section takes a look at the individual perpetrators of the school-based mass shootings occurring in the twenty-year period stretching from the shooting at Columbine High School (Littleton, Colorado) on April 20, 1999, through the shooting at Santa Fe High School (Santa Fe, Texas) on May 20, 2018. This involves eighteen perpetrators from seventeen school-based mass shooting incidents.[43] In some respects, the group was very similar in terms of gender and race. The overwhelming number of school-based mass shooters were white males. All the shooters were male, and 83% (*n=18*) were white. Another 11% were American Indian, with the remaining 6% African American. The perpetrators appear to be the most diverse when it comes to age. The youngest perpetrator was fourteen, and the oldest was fifty-three. However, that appearance of diversity is largely due to the age range. In fact, the majority of the perpetrators at 56% (*n=18*) were under the age of eighteen, with 50% (*n=10*) of the juvenile perpetrators being fifteen years old. Fifteen year olds were the dominant age group among all the perpetrators at 28% (n=*18*).

High schools were the dominant mass shooting location for 78% (*n=18*) of the perpetrators, elementary schools were the location for 17%, and 5% of the shootings were at a combination junior/senior high school. No mass shootings occurred at stand-alone junior high or middle schools in this twenty-year period. The three perpetrators who carried out mass shootings at elementary schools ranged in age from twenty to fifty-three. Two shooters had connections to the targeted elementary schools. Cedric Anderson's estranged wife was a teacher at the North Park Elementary School in San Bernardino, California. He was also the oldest perpetrator at fifty-three years old. Adam Lanza was a former student at the Sandy Hook Elementary School in Newtown, Connecticut. The remaining elementary school shooter, Charles C. Roberts, had no connection to the West Nickel Mines School. All the perpetrators in the high school mass shootings were current or former students.

The majority of perpetrators planned their shootings in advance, with 83% (*n=18*) known to have engaged in a degree of advance planning, some of it long-term. For many of the perpetrators, the plan also included a culminating suicide. One-half (*n=18*) committed suicide as the concluding act in the shooting incident. One perpetrator committed suicide in jail. Podlogar et al. have furthered the understanding of murder-suicide by stressing the need to focus less on typologies and more on predictive theories.[44] Podlogar et al. examined both stream and strain theories as applied to murder-suicide.[45]

Twenty-eight percent (*n=18*) of the perpetrators were believed to be fascinated by neo-Nazi or other white supremacist groups. Only 22% (*n=18*) had an actual mental health diagnosis, pre-shooting. Assuming the prevalence of mental health issues as a primary causal factor, this points to the large number of perpetrators who have "slipped through the cracks" in terms of a preexisting diagnosis, which might have led to effective intervention. Many of the perpetrators had complicated lives. In addition to any diagnosed or undiagnosed mental health issues, this may also include unstable family environments, trouble in school, law enforcement contact, and in many cases, extreme ideological ideations. These are the types of environmental factors that produce strain.

The remainder of this section explores a brief mix of environmental and individual factors for each of the school shooters. This type of exploration is always fraught with challenges. For instance, when half of the perpetrators have committed suicide, they are not available to provide insight into motivation, or perceptions of their personal school and family dynamics. The exploration is limited to open source, publically available information. A common problem is that in the initial aftermath, witness statements and media reports may not be accurate. However, once printed and repeatedly cited, this information then becomes the accepted canon making it harder to ascertain the truth.[46]

Eric Harris, Age Eighteen, & Dylan Klebold., Age Seventeen (Columbine High School—Littleton, Colorado)

It is ironic that the fame they sought will forever elude them as they will always be linked together. Even in a discussion of perpetrators, they almost merge into a third being. Both came from intact two-parent homes, with no known parental or family dysfunction.[47] Eric Harris was the son of an Air Force pilot and frequently moved until the move to Colorado in his adolescence.[48] Dylan Klebold came from an upper-middle-class home and was considered gifted.[49] When the lens shifts to the individual, the picture changes. Both had school problems and law enforcement encounters before the mass shooting. Both had previously been suspended from Columbine High School for computer hacking, and Dylan Klebold was also suspended for defacing a locker.[50] Both had previously been arrested for breaking into a van and stealing equipment.[51]

Despite initial reporting, neither were ostracized or failing in school.[52] In fact, they had friends and did fairly well in school.[53] On the day of the shootings, they wore trenchcoats, not because they were members of the "Trenchcoat Mafia" but to hide the pipebombs and firearms. What is disturbing were the missed warning signs. Law enforcement was aware that they were making bombs and threatening their friends, but the requested search warrant was never executed.[54] Two months before the attack, Dylan Klebold wrote an essay disturbing enough to alarm his teacher, who reported it to school officials.[55] Eric Harris's journals reveal that he hated the world and wanted to destroy it. Not because he felt victimized by it, but because he deeply felt that he was more powerful than the rest of the world.[56] The two shared a world view, which became reflected in a website describing their bombmaking activity, and where individuals were mentioned by name along with descriptions of horrible ways in which they would be murdered.[57] The existence of this website was known, as one of the listed victims saw himself on the website.[58]

It was initially believed that the attack took place on April 20 because that was Hitler's birthday, and both Eric Harris and Dylan Klebold were fans. In actuality, the attack was originally planned for April 19 on the anniversary of the Oklahoma City Bombing of the Edward Murrah Federal Building. The attack had to be delayed because the local drug dealer who was supposed to supply them with ammunition did not come through on time.[59] His journal writings suggest Eric Harris found a clear affinity with the genocidal nazi mania.[60] However, their admiration for the Oklahoma City Bombing also indicates far-right extremist ideations consistent with the worldview expressed in their writings.

T. J. Soloman, Age Fifteen (Heritage High School—Conyers, Georgia)

Exactly one month after Columbine, T. J. Soloman hit six students and two bookbags in a crowded school lobby with his stepfather's .22-caliber rifle.[61] No one was killed. T. J. Soloman lived with his mother and stepfather in a rural community in Georgia.[62] He had lost all contact with his father by the age of four, which he reportedly described as the worst thing that had ever happened to him.[63] A good student, his grades had recently dropped. There were anecdotal reports of depression. There were no previous reported incidents of problems with school or law enforcement.

He became obsessed with Columbine and had begun to talk about wanting to shoot up the school. He reportedly told a friend that the Columbine shooters could have killed more people if they had not stopped to aim at specific ones.[64] He put his stepfather/s handgun to his mouth in a suicide attempt but was stopped by the assistant principal. After being convicted and sentenced to forty years, the judge cut the sentence in half to twenty years for one aggravated assault charge.[65] After spending more than half in life in prison, T. J. Soloman was released in 2016 at the age of thirty-two and placed on psychiatric probation requiring continued mental health treatment for an additional twenty years.[66] T. J. Soloman also attempted suicide while in prison.[67]

Charles Andrew Williams, Age Fifteen (Santana High School—Santee, California)

Charles Andrew Williams planned his attack with two other students who backed out. Among the three of them, they told fifty additional people, including adults. His parents were divorced, living in different parts of the country. He lived with his father, visiting his mother, usually once a year.[68] He moved frequently. Initially, he did well in school, but as he approached adolescence, his performance declined. By that time, however, he was skipping school and abusing drugs and alcohol.[69] The school did attempt to notify his father by leaving a message on the home answering machine when he had not been in school. Charles Andrew Williams would erase the messages before his father arrived home from work.[70] He was sexually molested by an adult male. Charles Andrew Williams had at least one prior encounter with law enforcement when he was found with several 40 ounce bottles of beer.[71] No charges resulted from that encounter.

Charles Andrew Williams was physically small at fifteen. He later described frequent and severe bullying, including being lit on fire by his classmates. At the time of his arrest, however, he told police he had not been bullied.[72] After announcing the date of the shooting, he began to give away his possessions. This is often a marker for individuals contemplating suicide. Charles Andrew Williams later reported thinking about suicide but decided to do the shooting instead. Following the shooting, he put the gun to his head but was unable to pull the trigger. Following the attack that killed two and wounded thirteen, he was diagnosed as having a major depressive disorder.[73] Charles Andrew Williams is currently serving a fifty-year prison sentence.

Jason Hoffman, Age Eighteen (Granite Hill High School—El Cajon, California)

Jason Hoffman's difficulties began very early. As a toddler, he was abused by his father resulting in his father's arrest.[74] His father also assaulted his mother. In the tenth grade, Jason Hoffman was arrested for hitting a classmate with a racquet.[75] He had some academic difficulties, spent several years in special education, and repeated the twelfth grade.[76] Jason Hoffman also had a conflict with the dean of his high school, who is believed to have been the target of the shooting. Jason Hoffman had a history of mental illness. Prior to the shooting he had been diagnosed as clinically depressed and in need of medication. After the shooting, he told a probation officer that the reason for the shootings was that he wanted to commit "suicide by cop." This shooting also had no fatalities. Jason Hoffman killed himself in jail while awaiting trial.[77]

Jeffery Weise, Age Sixteen (Red Lake Senior High School—Red Lake, Minnesota)

Both parents were alcoholics, and both had repeated law enforcement contact. In what may have been foreshadowing, his father killed himself in an armed standoff with the police. His mother was jailed for driving while intoxicated, and for assault.[78] After his mother suffered brain damage in a car accident, Jeffery Weise's stepfather took his two children and left.[79] Jeffery Weise lived with various relatives and foster families. At the time of the shooting, he lived with his grandfather, who was a tribal police officer, and his grandfather's girlfriend. Jeffery Weise experienced multiple school failures. He repeated the eighth grade, and at the time of the shooting was on homebound instruction, although it is unclear exactly why he was out of school.[80] Jeffery Weise told several students about his plans to attack the school. Following the shooting, one student was arrested for conspiracy, but those charges were dropped. School officials were also aware of his violent journal entries about mass shootings. He is believed to have been interested in Hitler and the nazis.[81] Once engaged with law enforcement, Jeffery Weise went into a classroom and killed himself.

Charles C. Roberts, Age Thirty-Two (West Nickel Mines Amish School—West Nickel Mines, Pennsylvania)

Charles C. Roberts was married with three children. He had no prior history of mental health issues or violence. Despite that, he spent months stockpiling the supplies he would need for the initial hostage-taking and subsequent murders and suicide. The only clue is a call he made to his wife before shooting the students and committing suicide. In that call, he said that a girl had "wronged" him twenty years earlier. There is nothing to suggest any connection to the Amish community in this explanation.

Asa Coon, Age Fourteen (Success Tech Academy—Cleveland, Ohio)

In the space of two years, law enforcement visited Asa Coon's home five times for domestic violence, assault, property crime, and a hit-and-run.[82] Social services made visits to the house due to reports of scratches, burns, and flea bites on Asa Coon. His mother was the subject of a court neglect case, and he often went to school dirty and unkempt.[83] Nor was school a refuge. Asa Coon had at least two school suspensions. One suspension was the previous year for ten days. The second suspension was right before the shooting.[84] Asa Coon had law enforcement contacts as well. When he was twelve, he was charged with domestic violence for aggressive behavior toward his mother.[85] He had a previous suicide attempt and had spent time in a mental health facility. His most recent suspension was because of a fight. He was allegedly angry because the teachers would not listen to his side of the story. Police believe that Asa Coon targeted specific victims before going into an empty classroom and killing himself.

Robert Butler, Jr., Age Eighteen (Millard South High School—Omaha, Nebraska)

Robert Butler, Jr.'s father was a police detective in Omaha. Robert Butler, Jr. had received a criminal trespass citation for driving his car on the school's track and football field. He was called out of class to discuss the citation and received a long suspension.[86] After being escorted out of the building, he returned several hours later, specifically targeting the school official who had him escorted off the premises earlier in the day. His body was found an hour later, two miles away in the still-running car.

T. J. Lane, Age Seventeen (Chardon High School- Chardon, Ohio)

Both his parents had been charged with domestic violence. His mother had a drinking problem and was jailed for violent behavior. His father had multiple arrests for violent crimes. He was sent to prison for beating and kidnapping a woman.[87] By the time of the shooting incident, T. J. Lane had a visible pattern of escalating violent behavior. In separate incidents, T. J. Lane was charged with simple assault, and then a month later, he was charged with assault in another incident.[88] He was subsequently sent to an alternative high school. Following the shooting at his former school, he waited outside for the police to arrive to take him into custody. During the trial, he is reported to have mocked the victims' families. After pleading guilty, he was sentenced to three life sentences without parole.

Adam Lanza, Age Twenty (Sandy Hook Elementary School—Newtown, Connecticut)

Adam Lanza's parents were divorced, and he had limited, if any, contact with his father and brother prior to the shooting. He lived in the basement of his mother's home and, for a period of time, only communicated with her via email. He changed schools several times before being homeschooled by his mother.[89] He was fixated on guns. A gun enthusiast herself, Adam Lanza's mother, is believed to have encouraged this hobby as a way of providing a shared interest. She is believed, however, to have been unaware of the extent of his fixation.[90] It was a fixation that extended to mass murder. Following the shooting, law enforcement investigators found a 7 x 4 foot spreadsheet in 9 point font (that even required a special printer) where he listed the details of all previous successful and attempted mass killings. Investigators believe that he wanted to be at the top of this list.[91] An obsessive video gamer, his actions during the shooting resembled a live-action video game in the manner in which he carried out the shooting.[92] Adam Lanza killed his mother before heading to the school. He killed himself at the school.

Jaylen Fryberg, Age Fifteen (Marysville Pilchuck High School—Marysville, Washington)

Jaylen Fryberg was a good student and was very involved in his tribe and played sports. His primary hobby was hunting, and he often received guns for his birthday from his father. His father worked for the Tulalip Tribal Natural Resources Department and was respected for trying to preserve tribal customs.[93] His mother was a member of the Marysville School District Board of Directors.[94] He was bullied for being an American Indian. Shortly before the attack, Jaylen Fryberg was suspended from the football team for fighting.[95] He sent messages to his friends, asking them to meet him for lunch. He shot his friends, some of whom were his cousins, as they were seated at the cafeteria table for lunch before he shot himself. Jaylen Fryberg was the only perpetrator to deliberately target their friends. In writings that were found,

Jaylen Fryberg had written that he needed his crew with him. Just prior to the shooting, he sent a suicide note to his family. Jaylen Fryberg took the gun from his father's truck where it was stored.[96] Due to a prior domestic charge, his father was actually prohibited from owning guns. Federal prosecutors subsequently charged Jaylen Fryberg's father with unlawful possession.[97]

James "Austin" Hancock, Age Fourteen (Madison High School—Middletown, Ohio)

James "Austin" Hancock was born when his parents were in high school.[98] His mother later served time in jail on a drug charge. His father had custody since he was four years old. James "Austin" Hancock lived with his father, stepmother, and siblings. He had recently begun arguing with his father over his grades. Several months before taking the gun to school, he had written a suicide note that he later flushed down the toilet.[99] On the day of the shooting, he showed the gun to several students, one of whom was on her way to tell authorities.[100] James "Austin" Hancock did not want to go back home, so he started shooting. There was no specific target. Two of the students who were shown the gun (both fourteen-year-old boys) were charged with failure to report a crime.[101] James "Austin" Hancock was charged with four counts of attempted murder and inducing panic. He was sentenced to a juvenile detention facility until the age of twenty-one.[102]

Cedric Anderson, Age Fifty-three (North Park Elementary School—San Bernardino, California)

This was a domestic violence incident ending in murder-suicide. Cedric Anderson had a history of violence against women. Two women (other than his estranged wife) had restraining orders against him. Previous charges for brandishing a firearm had been dropped. His estranged wife had previously shared her concerns about his behavior with her family.

Caleb Sharpe, Age Fifteen (Freeman High School—Rockford, Washington)

Caleb Sharpe was under the care of the school counselor for having suicidal thoughts.[103] He had bragged to his friends about owning multiple guns. Caleb Sharpe was obsessed with school shootings and had made multiple YouTube videos about school shootings where he was firing his guns. He had drawn Xs in the school yearbook on the pictures of his targets. Caleb Sharpe had been suspended earlier in the school year after a plan he had written for a school shooting was found by another student and turned over to school officials. He was later allowed to return to school. After killing the student who bullied him and firing three random shots that wounded three other students, Caleb Sharpe stopped when he was confronted by the school janitor. He indicated to the police that he was not targeting anyone but wanted to teach his classmates a lesson about what happens when you bully people. He had taken the weapons from his father's gun safe.[104] His father knew that he had the combination to the safe.

Gabriel Ross Parker, Age Fifteen (Marshall County Junior/Senior High School—Benton, Kentucky)

Gabriel Ross Parker killed two people and injured eighteen. He played the trombone in the school band. Gabriel Ross Parker believed that neither his life nor anyone else's had any meaning and reportedly planned the shooting as an experiment to see how students, the police, and society would react.[105] Immediately before the shooting, he took the time to make sure that his fellow band members would be safe.[106] In the months before the shooting, Gabriel Ross Parker had made online threats against some students.[107] He was allegedly known to be obsessed with guns, World War II, and the Nazi regime.[108]

Nikolas Cruz, Age Nineteen (Marjory Stoneman Douglas High School—Parkland, Florida)

By middle school, his teachers recognized that Nikolas Cruz was profoundly disturbed and obsessed with hurting others.[109] He was eventually transferred to a more therapeutic school for emotionally and behaviorally disturbed children.[110] He did well at that school but did not want to stay. He was permitted to enroll in Marjorie Stoneman Douglas. He did not do well there. One school year, he was suspended eighteen times. Academically he was failing his classes. Nikolas Cruz threatened to rape and kill another student.[111] He had a history of attempted suicide and depression. One time he live-streamed slitting his wrists on the internet. He was investigated by the FBI for his online postings about school shootings. Records show that after misleading him into giving up his special education status, school officials pressured him into withdrawing from school.[112] His adoptive mother had died three months before the shooting (his adoptive father had previously died), and he had moved in with friends of the family.[113] They knew he owned an AR-15 and made him keep it locked up in a cabinet, for which they also knew he had a key.[114]

Dimitrios Pagourtzis, Age Seventeen (Santa Fe High School—Santa Fe, Texas)

Dimitrios Pagourtzis posted online about "being born to kill" complete with pictures of neo-Nazi paraphernalia and symbols of other alt-right organizations and movements.[115] Other images on his subsequently deleted Facebook page suggests that he also may have been interested in white supremacist organizations.[116] He deliberately refrained from shooting students he liked so they "could tell his story." After the shooting, IEDs (Improvised Explosive Devices) were found at the school and at Dimitrios Pagourtzis' home. He has been found incompetent to stand trial and during the writing of this book has been confined to a state mental facility in Texas.[117]

CONCLUSION

A mentally healthy individual does not engage in a mass shooting. For that matter, neither do the overwhelming number of individuals with mental health challenges. This chapter presented several different types of explanations for why a number of persons do perpetrate school-based mass shootings. A theme of "missed opportunities" runs through many of these perpetrator synopses. Missed opportunity for intervention to prevent the shooting. Missed opportunity for intervention to mitigate the underlying contributing factors. Comparing perpetrator factors to theoretical explanations, models, and typologies can broaden our understanding of this phenomenon.

NOTES

1. (McGinty et al. 2014).
2. See (Fox and Harding 2005).
3. (Metzl and MacLeish 2015).
4. (Metzl and MacLeish 2015).
5. (Mingus and Zopf 2010).
6. (Skeem and Mulvey 2020).
7. (Skeem and Mulvey 2020).
8. (Skeem and Mulvey 2020).
9. (Aseltine Jr., Gore and Gordon 2000).
10. (Blum and Jaworski 2016).
11. (Aseltine Jr., Gore and Gordon 2000).
12. (Lemieux 2014).
13. (Lemieux 2014).
14. (Langman 2010).

15. (Langman 2017).
16. (Rice and Hoffman 2015).
17. (Rice and Hoffman 2015).
18. (Lupica 2013).
19. (Newman et al. 2008).
20. (Lenhardt, Farrell and Graham 2010).
21. (Lenhardt, Farrell and Graham 2010).
22. (Welton, Vakil and Ford 2014).
23. (Fox and Harding 2005).
24. (Fox and Harding 2005).
25. (Fox and Harding 2005).
26. (Fox and Harding 2005).
27. (O'Toole 2000).
28. (Ioannou, Hammond and Simpson 2015). Ioannou et al. used Smallest Space Analysis to study the co-occurrence of these risk factors. The result was a two-dimensional plot with the risk factors grouped into readily identifiable distinct regions.
29. The percentages do not add up to 100 because some cases could not be placed in a category (Ioannou, Hammond and Simpson 2015).
30. (Farr 2018).
31. (Farr 2018).
32. (Farr 2018).
33. (O'Toole 2000).
34. (O'Toole 2000).
35. (O'Toole 2000).
36. (Lenhardt, Farrell and Graham 2010).
37. (Osborne and Capellan 2016).
38. (Osborne and Capellan 2016).
39. (Osborne and Capellan 2016).
40. (Osborne and Capellan 2016).
41. (Osborne and Capellan 2016).
42. (Osborne and Capellan 2016).
43. (Lane Pixley and Flowers 2019). Unless otherwise indicated, all descriptive, numerical, and statistical information presented came from that consolidated dataset.
44. (Podlogar et al. 2018).
45. (Podlogar et al. 2018).
46. (Lane Pixley and Flowers 2019). Unless otherwise indicated, the perpetrator and incident information comes from the consolidated dataset used for this study, described earlier, where the information from the dataset has been supplemented, that is indicated.
47. (Langman, Education: Failures and Family Involvement ver 1.10 2017).
48. (Margaritoff 2019).
49. (Margaritoff 2019).
50. (Langman, Education: Failures and Family Involvement ver 1.10 2017).
51. (Langman, Legal Histories of School Shooters ver. 1.3 2018).
52. (Margaritoff 2019).

53. (Gumbel 2009).
54. (Gumbel 2009).
55. (Gumbel 2009).
56. (Margaritoff 2019).
57. (Margaritoff 2019).
58. (Margaritoff 2019).
59. (Gumbel 2009).
60. (Gumbel 2009).
61. (Eldridge 2016).
62. (Eldridge 2016).
63. (Langman, School Shooters: The Myth of the Stable Home ver. 1.15 2016).
64. (Farr 2018).
65. (Eldridge 2016).
66. (Eldridge 2016).
67. (Langman, School Shooters: A Miscellany ver 1.35 2018).
68. (Dickey 2013).
69. (Dickey 2013).
70. (Dickey 2013).
71. (Langman, Legal Histories of School Shooters ver. 1.3 2018).
72. (Dickey 2013).
73. (Dickey 2013).
74. (Langman, School Shooters: The Myth of the Stable Home ver. 1.15 2016).
75. (Langman, Legal Histories of School Shooters ver. 1.3 2018).
76. (Langman, Education: Failures and Family Involvement ver 1.10 2017).
77. (B. Fox 2001).
78. (Langman, School Shooters: The Myth of the Stable Home ver. 1.15 2016).
79. (Langman, School Shooters: The Myth of the Stable Home ver. 1.15 2016).
80. (Langman, Education: Failures and Family Involvement ver 1.10 2017).
81. (Langman, School Shooters: A Miscellany ver 1.35 2018).
82. (Langman, School Shooters: The Myth of the Stable Home ver. 1.15 2016).
83. (Langman, School Shooters: The Myth of the Stable Home ver. 1.15 2016).
84. (Langman, Education: Failures and Family Involvement ver 1.10 2017).
85. (Langman, Legal Histories of School Shooters ver. 1.3 2018).
86. (Langman, Education: Failures and Family Involvement ver 1.10 2017).
87. (Langman, School Shooters: The Myth of the Stable Home ver. 1.15 2016).
88. (Langman, Legal Histories of School Shooters ver. 1.3 2018).
89. (Langman, Education: Failures and Family Involvement ver 1.10 2017).
90. (Lupica 2013).
91. (Lupica 2013).
92. (Lupica 2013).
93. (Kutner 2015).
94. (Kutner 2015).
95. (Langman, Education: Failures and Family Involvement ver 1.10 2017).
96. (Langman, The Origins of Firearms Used in School Shootings in the United States ver. 1.1 2016).

97. (Kutner 2015).
98. (Biery Golick 2017).
99. (Biery Golick 2017).
100. (Pack 2016).
101. (Pack 2016).
102. (Pack 2016).
103. (CBS News AP 2017).
104. (CBS News AP 2017).
105. (Wolfson 2019).
106. (Wolfson 2019).
107. (Riley 2019).
108. (Riley 2019).
109. (Wallman and O'Matz 2019).
110. (Wallman and O'Matz 2019).
111. (Wallman and O'Matz 2019).
112. (Wallman and O'Matz 2019).
113. (Kennedy 2018).
114. (Kennedy 2018).
115. (Weill and Briquelet 2018).
116. (Weill and Briquelet 2018).
117. (Powell 2019).

Chapter 7

Public Policy Considerations

INTRODUCTION

Guns. The single word is charged with emotion. It is so charged with emotion that its very mention can inhibit the ability to effectively debate public policy strategies. The choice is frequently presented as a binary one: guns or no guns. But perhaps the question is more nuanced. Perhaps it is a version of how to let everyone have the type of firearm that they want, along with the ability to carry it when and where they want, while simultaneously keeping firearms away from those who may wish to harm themselves or others. This chapter discusses the public policy concerns arising from issues previously discussed in this book. These concerns are organized into two main thematic areas: legal and institutional/organizational. As will be seen below, there is a good deal of overlap in the application of these areas. The legal area includes state and local laws, policies, and regulations, while the institutional/organizational area is school-based, and looks at programmatic thrusts. This chapter will briefly illustrate challenges or approaches in each of these areas.

Public policy is often conceived as a linear progression. A policy is expressly developed, and the implementing action subsequently follows. Often, however, an incident occurs, followed by governmental action in response. The justification for the "policy" underlying the governmental response is developed during or after the implementation of that response. A school-based mass shooting is an example of the type of situation where response sometimes precedes policy development. This is understandable. Something has happened. Something horrendous. But, in the absence of informed debate and discussions of alternatives and the implications of the proposed action, then school districts as well as state and local governments can find themselves having expended sums of money on ineffective efforts. Once dollars start flowing, it is almost impossible to turn off the faucet.

The most common approach to securing schools from mass shooters are changes associated with their physical structure. There are two types of perpetrators. Those mass shooters who have targeted elementary schools are not students but are coming in from outside the school. The best strategy for this type of perpetrator is to harden the exterior to make it harder for them to enter. This strategy is followed by schools at all levels. To delineate the difference between those strategies and what is proposed in this chapter, the chapter will begin with a brief overview of two such approaches. It should be noted that the responses described below occurred in jurisdictions that were not the site of a school-based mass shooting incident.

Immediately following the shooting at Santa Fe High School (Santa Fe, Texas), a small school district, with less than 2,000 students, began developing a multipronged strategy.[1] They added security cameras and applied bullet-resistant film to windows. They hardened classroom doors with bolts and remote locking devices. They invested in software to constantly search the web for mention of the school district and in assault weapons for their added security personnel.[2] As a matter of policy, their investments were in hardware, software, and armed security officers. These are investments that can be seen, and this is a common approach. It is focused on stopping or deterring the *bad act*. It is, however, distinct from addressing the underlying reasons for the act.

Following the shootings at Marjory Stoneman Douglas High School (Parkland, Florida), one technology company offered its facial recognition technology to K–12 schools for free to upgrade their in-school security systems.[3] Other companies have also entered the market. As may be expected, this is a controversial strategy. In addition to the discomfort, many parents may feel over the intrusive nature of the surveillance of their children the entire time they are in school; there are other concerns as well. The concerns are two-pronged: the software itself and the use to which the software can be put.

A substantial concern directed toward the underlying algorithms that comprise the software is that facial recognition software has documented issues in reading darker skin tones.[4] There is a concern about potentially criminalizing black and brown students if these systems are linked to local law enforcement. The concern flows from potential identification problems caused by the algorithm, as well as from the disciplinary disparities, which are discussed below. There are also concerns that some parents will be reluctant to come to schools that are outfitted with facial recognition cameras, particularly if they are undocumented or have other legal issues.

This would automatically decrease the parental involvement with schools that is so crucial and is also described below. There is concern that parents viewed as troublesome by teachers and administrators have been placed on watch lists and barred from schools (under threat of arrest).[5] Facial recognition systems do offer benefits for schools. They have detected instances of a noncustodial parent leaving with a child. These systems have caught pedophiles who wondered into a school. The question which should have been subject to a robust public policy debate was whether the benefits outweighed the disadvantages.

LEGAL

In the legal area, there are two approach trajectories. These trajectories either focus on the external school environment, or they focus on the internal school environment. The effectiveness of existing gun laws and restrictions as well as the need for additional ones continue to be debated. In reality, however, the perpetrator demographic for many of these school-based mass shootings will continue to fly under the radar screen. Many students are getting their weapons from home, from their parents' gun closets. They live in jurisdictions with a strong gun culture, so they may have experiences hunting or on the gun range. They are familiar with and comfortable with guns. These perpetrators are not the demographic typically envisioned when discussions occur on the subject of removing guns from "violent offenders." Most of the adolescents did not have a preexisting mental health diagnosis, so they would not be subject to exclusion on that basis either.

External School Environment

One trajectory, leading to either a reduction in the number of incidents of school-based mass shootings or reduced fatalities when those incidents occur, is to reduce the availability of guns in the wider environment within which schools exist or limit access to those guns. Cook et al. highlighted the need to penalize straw purchasers of firearms to disincentivize this practice. In theory, this might have discouraged Adam Lanza's mother, who made straw purchases of weapons for her son that were later used at Sandy Hook Elementary School. It might also have discouraged the female classmate who made the straw purchase for Eric Harris and Dylan Klebold before Columbine. Cook et al. however were focused on the larger issue of gun violence as it plays out daily in American life. Their target was to reduce access to guns by violent offenders.[6] A white suburban mother making a straw purchase of a firearm for her son most likely does not appear on the radar screen. A white middle-class teenage girl making a straw purchase of what she thought was a weapon for hunting does not appear on the radar screen either. Nor does a father in a rural area buying guns to encourage his son's love of hunting.

As a practical matter, these types of purchases are the mechanism by which many of the school shooters obtained or had access to the weapons they used. In each of these instances, the resulting carnage had a much higher level of fatalities than shooting someone in a robbery attempt. Developing a strategy for reducing this practice would serve the purpose of keeping weapons out of the hands of vulnerable young people. Brown et al. argue that raising the age to own long guns from eighteen to twenty-one would have reduced the number of incidents and the resulting number of fatalities.[7] This strategy, however, conflicts with American's love of their guns. It also assumes that the shooter did not have an available gun in their home that may have belonged to someone else.

Every school-based mass shooting generates new cries to strengthen the background check system, particularly red flag laws. To increase the reporting of disqualified individuals to NICS, the Social Security Administration planned to report to NICS the names of the recipients of Social Security Disability payments who were mentally impaired and incapable of managing their finances. The rules were finalized in the last days of the Obama administration. It is possible to see the logic in the reasoning that if an individual is mentally impaired and incapable of managing their finances, then they probably should not have a firearm. Congress took the rare step of repealing this rule less than two months later, after the swearing-in of a House of Representatives, and a Senate, both dominated by republicans. While there may be a desire to conclude that Congress took that action after a judicious weighing of the competing interests involved, it was not clear if that was the case. It is worth noting that this Congressional action was hailed by groups as diverse as the National Rifle Association (NRA) and the American Civil Liberties Union (ACLU). Mental health groups were split.

There is a danger when mass shootings are assumed to be the result of serious mental illness.[8] Skeem et al. argued that, since violence is a multidimensional problem, a gun policy directed toward keeping guns out of the hands of those with mental illness would not reduce mass shootings and would only further stigmatize those individuals.[9] This is a fairly consistent position. Podlogar et al. when discussing the closely aligned area of murder-suicide as juxtaposed with efforts to add even more mentally disabled individuals to the prohibited purchaser lists in the NICS database, described the policies as either imprecise and stigmatizing, or misdirected and ineffective.[10]

Effective use of red flag laws also requires serious consideration of whether the restriction should extend to the household and not simply to the individual. These laws preclude individuals from purchasing a firearm based on factors such as a prior domestic assault, felony drug conviction, dangerousness to self (usually triggered if an individual is suicidal). These are more fully described in chapter 2. These are exclusions based on behavior. Excluding individuals suffering from a mental illness, solely because of their status as mentally disabled, is essentially excluding a group of people based on what they are rather than what they have done. This practice would seem to violate the equal protection and due process clauses of the U.S. Constitution.

It can be argued that to maintain an arsenal of firearms in a household, which includes an individual who has previously attempted suicide, is at best an unnecessary temptation and at worst cruel. The issue raised when maintaining those weapons in a household that includes an individual who has previously committed violent acts is it would arguably create, at minimum, moral complicity in acts committed with those weapons. Locking the weapons in a gun cabinet has repeatedly been demonstrated to be ineffective. It is recognized that this is, in effect, penalizing an individual whose behavior would not otherwise subject them to regulation. To do otherwise negates the ban on the restricted individual as they would still have easy access to the firearms they are prohibited from purchasing.

In lieu of red flag laws, which would impose a blanket prohibition on all persons with a mental illness, Skeem et al. focused on "dangerousness," advocating for a strategy to keep guns away from all dangerous people, which would have the additional benefit of keeping them from the seriously mentally ill. "Dangerousness" as the operational term can be as problematic as focusing exclusively on mental illness. Is "dangerous" only referring to individuals who have demonstrated violent behavior, or does it also extend to those who have been identified as possessing imprecise pre-violence indicator tendencies? It can be a standard that, if it is left vague, has the potential to implicate the race and class fissures, which underlie any discussion of danger, violence, or crime.

Internal School Environment

Concurrent with, or as an alternative to reducing the availability of guns in the wider environment, is the need to ensure guns do not get into the schools. School districts have invested significant sums of money on metal detectors and additional security to harden school perimeters. They then see it rendered useless when a perpetrator pulls a fire alarm causing the students to exit the building where they are then shot. Gaining traction on the legal front has been the argument to arm faculty and staff either expressly or by allowing them the ability to carry their own concealed weapons on school property. On hearing about proposals to arm school teachers as a way to respond to school-based shootings, one high school teacher in a major urban area responded in frustration and exasperation, "I have enough trouble making sure my purse doesn't get stolen, now they want me to keep track of a gun as well?"[11]

In most jurisdictions, schools are "gun-free" zones. In recent years, it has increasingly been argued that permitting concealed carry on school premises by teachers and staff would either (1) reduce the occurrence of school-based mass shootings or (2) quickly terminate them when they occurred.[12] This argument also advocates the reduction or elimination of gun-free zones. The argument relies on the belief that if a potential shooter knew that they might confront armed resistance, then they would be less likely to attack a school. This assumes a rational perpetrator, something that has not been supported by the cases reviewed. The reality is that individuals with a concealed carry permit are already able to carry weapons on school premises, although standards, training, even disclosure requirements vary from jurisdiction to jurisdiction.[13] Minshew's concern is with the impact that arming teachers would have on school climate and particularly the impact on students of color.[14]

This is not a trivial concern. A 2018 report by the Government Accountability Office (GAO) found that serious disciplinary disparities existed for black students, boys, and students with disabilities. American Indians/Alaskan Natives were also overrepresented. However, the greatest disparities were for black students. These disciplinary disparities included actions such as in-school suspension, out-of-school suspension, expulsion, corporal punishment, referral to law enforcement, and school-related arrests. Black students represented 15.5% of the student population, but they accounted for 39% of all school suspensions.[15] Girls were underrepresented in disciplinary actions. However, black girls were overrepresented. Nineteen percent of students with disabilities were black, but they accounted for 36% of students with disabilities who were suspended from school.[16] These disparities start in preschool and are consistent regardless of the poverty level of the school, the grade level of the school, or the type of public school.[17] When you factor in teachers with guns and factor in the impact of unconscious bias, the situation is ripe for students to be shot by teachers. It is this type of hostile climate to which Minshew refers.[18] Not addressed are the liability issues that would arise when a teacher shot a student who "appeared dangerous" but was not.

At its most basic, a school-based mass shooting is a crime. Crime and delinquency are viewed through a lens tinted by color and class. Most studies of delinquency have focused on the delinquency of the "lower classes." Criminal is often a synonym for a person of color, even though every study of self-reported juvenile behavior indicates the same levels of self-reported delinquency across class and color lines. In regards to school-based mass shootings, this has had profound consequences. When theoretical explanations for delinquency are utilized to examine juveniles from primarily middle-class homes in suburban or rural communities, they can be seen to exhibit the same anomic behavior, the same alienation, and the same aimlessness that is readily identified in the children of the poor. Because nonurban living is often viewed through an idyllic frame, young people whose home conditions are not the stable family environment pictured for suburban and rural communities are overlooked; their needs unmet. Their parents *don't look like people who abuse their children* (emphasis added). So questions are not asked, and a child's trauma intensifies.

Reviews of perpetrators' backgrounds that are enabled through open-source materials reveal, in many cases, young people as fragile and as much in need as their urban, less-advantaged, or minority counterparts. Distinct from the picture of the assault rifle wielding older adolescent or young adult male, the perpetrator seen most frequently is a fourteen-year-old or fifteen-year-old adolescent. In personality, motivation, and outcomes, they are different from their seventeen to twenty-year-old counterparts. This is a clear example where the colorization of delinquency has adverse effects on those who do not fit the expected picture. It highlights the importance of seeking solutions before a school-based mass shooting incident occurs.

INSTITUTIONAL/ORGANIZATIONAL

Traditionally, strategies and solutions have focused on an approach that addresses only one piece of the problem. Solutions are discussed as if they are competing and as if only one can be implemented. Continuing this approach ensures that solutions will continue to elude. Effective responses require that we "walk and chew gum at the same time." In other words, it is necessary to adopt a holistic approach addressing multiple facets of the problem simultaneously. This approach is supported by the work of Ruggles et al. To understand the behavioral factors associated with youth gun possession, they looked at ten years' worth of data from the Center for Disease Control's (CDC) Youth Risk Behavior Surveillance System. Their findings led them to conclude that progress would not be made by continuing to treat one risk factor at a time.[19] As a result, Ruggles et al. advocated a shift to a more holistic "whole child" approach, such as a comprehensive school-based approach that included the development of positive coping mechanisms, socioemotional skills, risk assessment, and emotion regulation strategies to increase thoughtfulness and reduce impulsivity.[20]

Rice et al. reached a similar conclusion in terms of the need to adopt a multidirectional strategy. Their focus was on adolescents with a demonstrated inability to attain normative developmental goals.[21] For this population, it was believed that a dual strategy was required to prevent future mass shootings: not only gun removal from the home but also targeted treatment.[22] Rice et al. found that the common strategy of simply removing guns from the home would be ineffective. It would need to be coupled with supportive services.[23]

Lenhardt et al. recommended that schools: (1) adopt an ongoing assessment model, (2) provide sufficient staff and resources to implement the model, (3) reduce school size, (4) build communication infrastructures, (5) build collaboration with parents and the community, (6) build (bullying) prevention programs into the curriculum, and (7) expand the mission of the school to include social and emotional curricula.[24] Their study of fifteen targeted school shooters found that the interaction between a range of complex variables in a student's life was the underlying cause of targeted school violence. While variables related to personality factors and family dynamics were viewed as outside the control of the school, these recommendations address environmental factors or contextual variables that are within the school's control. They were blunt in their warning that a school's failure to control the environmental factors exacerbates the student's stress levels adding to the potential for violence.[25]

The need to reduce the underlying stressors that produce strain by addressing the social factors and the social environment was also addressed by Blum et al. They argued that it was important that potentially alienated young males be reintegrated into positive and supportive social environments before they commit mass shootings.[26] Welton et al. in his studies of rampage shooters advocated for proactive school-based interaction that expressly incorporated nonacademic issues such as family dysfunction.[27] As with the findings from many studies, this appears to assume a level of school psychologists and counselors who are not present at many public schools. Their absence ties back to Lenhardt's second recommendation, provision of sufficient staff and resources.

Bullying is often identified as a factor in the backgrounds of the perpetrators. It is important that bullying is addressed in schools. Bullying should never be discounted. It is worth keeping in mind that bullying has been a phenomenon as long as children (and adults for that matter) have interacted. What has changed over time has been the access of children to weapons that have become increasingly lethal. Additionally, schools are confronted with more behavioral issues resulting from trauma as well as other mental health issues.[28] Overly focusing on bullying behavior can sometimes overlook the problem causing the behavior. Bullying can signal a problem with the student who is the bully, as well as be a problem for the student being bullied. School officials reported in interviews with the Government Accounting Office (GAO) that as a result of increases in experienced trauma, their elementary school students were exhibiting aggressive behavior, which by the time they reached middle school had become self-destructive behavior.[29] In other words, the act of bullying may be the visible manifestation of underlying issues that need to be addressed.

Assuming that this range of student issues does delve onto the school for action, the question also arises: "Who" is responsible for "what"? In promoting a public health intervention response to violence in schools, King focused on the role of the school nurse in implementing a primary, secondary, and tertiary intervention model.[30] King saw the role of primary prevention as centered around facilitating communications between the school, community, parents, and students. It involves implementing educational programs for parents and students on issues such as conflict resolution and gun safety with the overall goal of creating a supportive climate for all students.[31]

King's secondary prevention level is directed toward the identification of students who are *at risk* for behavior problems.[32] This includes screening for domestic violence and regular health assessments. This level is targeted toward identifying those students who may be witnessing or experiencing violence.[33] A key component at the secondary prevention level is the active adult presence in places where students congregate, such as hallways, buses, and so on as a way to reduce bullying behavior. King envisioned the tertiary prevention level as focused on providing services both within the school and through community service agencies, as needed, to students who exhibited signs of school behavior problems.

The value of this type of strategy is that it does not begin when a problem becomes visible, which can often minimize the likelihood of successful intervention. It offers the advantage of addressing the needs of the very few students who may suffer from a serious mental illness, as well as the students whose behavior is a reaction to their social and environmental milieu producing mental health needs such as stress and anxiety. It has the potential to meet all students at the level of their individual need. King's proposal functions almost as a tiered triage approach. As a practical matter, this type of prevention model could be implemented not only by the school nurse but also by a school counselor or social worker. However, as with the previous recommendations, it suffers from the declining government investment in the type of educational resources most likely to benefit students.

The value-added of this model is that it envisions a public health or mental health professional intimately involved in the daily activity of the school and students. They appear to function as a part of the classroom team as a partner to the classroom teacher. This is important because often all new initiatives land squarely on the classroom teacher to be responsible for implementing, even as that teacher struggles with the increased challenges of carrying out their teaching responsibilities with increased class sizes and declining resources. This should not be read as to negate the role and importance of the classroom teacher.

Students often spend more of their waking hours at school than they do at home. This means that it is time to abandon the outdated notion that some things are parent responsibilities. While schools do not have any connection to things that occur in a student's life outside of school, the reality is that it is within the school that the consequences of those external occurrences are acted out. Therefore, schools of the twenty-first century must be proactive in engaging families and students. It is the teacher who typically first notices warning signs or red flags, not necessarily of impending violent behavior, but rather of a troubled child who may be experiencing trauma. Teachers need the training to know what to do when they read disturbing student work assignments. Schools need the resources so that when a teacher spots a warning sign, there is a nonpunitive intervention approach and another professional or paraprofessional ready to step in to engage intervention efforts.

Sometimes boys just like to talk about guns and mayhem and destruction. There is a level of masculine posturing that occurs when they are together. Most teachers are female. Most teachers are also white. The students sometimes are not. This dichotomy, coupled with subliminal biases, can create situations where students are inappropriately flagged as dangerous or disturbed. Teachers need the training (as the initial observer) to be able to distinguish between normal (albeit inappropriate) behavior and behavior that is concerning.

CONCLUSION

The inescapable conclusion is that when all of the rhetoric over this issue has settled, the guns came from home. With minimal exceptions, all of the weapons used in school-based mass shootings over the past twenty years have been legally acquired and have come from the perpetrator's home. Several students took guns from locked gun cabinets to which they had access. This suggests the gun cabinets functioned more to keep the guns out of the hands of intruding strangers than out of the hands of children already in the home. Young people struggling with an inability to handle a potential range of life stressors, who live in gun-supportive cultures and environments are even more vulnerable to potentially hurting themselves or hurting someone else.

The second inescapable conclusion is that for many of these shooters, behaviors were only identifiable in hindsight after the fact, as they were at the time indistinguishable from what is perceived to be typical adolescent angst. What this means is that families are often not aware until something has happened, and the pieces are put together that there was a problem. We can ask schools to "step up to the plate" and roll out the type of robust support and intervention services that students need. But since some things are only visible in hindsight, ultimately, as a society, we will need to address the question of how easy it should be for a fourteen- or fifteen-year old to access a gun, the type of gun they should be able to access, or the circumstances under which they should be able to access it.

Many believe that the search for solutions would be farther along, but for the 1996 prohibition against the Center for Disease Control (CDC) funding research that could be seen as promoting gun control. Skeem et al. noted that this ban had created a void for both practitioners and policy-makers, leaving an absence of empirical evidence upon which to base policy recommendations.[34] Despite this, people continue to try.

NOTES

1. (Simonite 2019).
2. (Simonite 2019).
3. (Nickelsburg and Moreno 2018).
4. (Simonite 2019).
5. (Simonite 2019).
6. (Cook and Pollack 2017).
7. (Brown and Goodin 2018).
8. (Skeem and Mulvey 2020).
9. (Skeem and Mulvey 2020).
10. (Podlogar et al. 2018).
11. (Anonymous 2019).
12. (Nedzel 2014).
13. (Minshew 2018).
14. (Minshew 2018).
15. (Government Accounting Office 2018).
16. (Government Accounting Office 2018).
17. (Government Accounting Office 2018).
18. (Minshew 2018).
19. (Ruggles and Rajan 2014).
20. (Ruggles and Rajan 2014).
21. (Rice and Leon 2015).
22. (Rice and Leon 2015).
23. (Rice and Leon 2015).
24. (Lenhardt, Farrell and Graham 2010).
25. (Lenhardt, Farrell and Graham 2010).
26. (Blum and Jaworski 2016).
27. (Welton, Vakil and Ford 2014).
28. (Lombardo and Turner 2018).

29. (Lombardo and Turner 2018).
30. (King 2014).
31. (King 2014).
32. (King 2014).
33. (King 2014).
34. (Skeem and Mulvey 2020).

Conclusion

The examination of twenty years of school-based mass shootings from Columbine to Santa Fe explored the larger environmental framework within which these incidents occurred. This examination yielded two inescapable conclusions. The first is that the increased number of fatalities in school-based mass shootings was due to the increased lethality of the weapons that are available to young people. The second is that those school-based mass shootings, which did not involve the use of assault weapons, had markedly fewer fatalities. However, approximately two-thirds of the school-based mass shootings incidents in the post-Columbine era involved the use of assault weapons. Often a single perpetrator carried multiple weapons. These incidents have occurred against the backdrop of a national policy, which has shifted from the regulation of firearms to the regulation of individuals.

School-based mass shootings were more likely to occur in states that had two characteristics. They did not ban assault weapons, and they did not have a minimum age for purchase or possession of long guns. A supportive regional gun culture plays a role in the occurrence of these incidents, but the aspect of that supportive culture that appears to be most directly tied to school-based mass shootings was the leisure-time use of guns. Regions that ranked high on leisure-time use of guns, such as the West and Midwest, had a larger number of incidents, although lower average fatalities per incident. Homicide is spontaneous, enabled by gun availability, and is both culturally and geographically concentrated.[1] It is not surprising that for young people, who spend much of their time in schools, that action is centered on schools. What was surprising was that fatalities ran in an inverse manner in relation to the number of incidents. As the number of incidents in a region increased, its average fatalities decreased. The Southern and Northeastern regions had the exact opposite pattern from the West and Midwest regions. The South and Northeast had a lower number of incidents, but a higher number of fatalities.

Also distinctive were aspects of the perpetrators. The typical high school shooter in the South and Northeast was eighteen to nineteen years of age. The typical high school shooter in the West and Midwest was fourteen to fifteen years of age. Often too young to buy weapons, these high school shooters in the West and Midwest brought them from home. This age difference is important. There are differences between a fourteen- or fifteen-year old and an eighteen- or nineteen-year old. This age difference also affected the characteristics of the incidents. The younger shooters, even when they also used semiautomatic weapons, did not kill as many people as their older counterparts. It is not clear why this was the case. Despite their familiarity with the weapons, because of their age they may have been less experienced. Or it may have had something to do with the fact that many of the younger shooters concluded their mass shootings by either successful or attempted suicide. In contrast, none of the high school shooters in the Southern region attempted suicide. They either fled, attempted to flee, or eventually surrendered.

The higher number of incidents in the West and Midwest, despite the younger age of the shooters, is connected to those regions' leisure-time use that generated familiarity, comfort, and most importantly access in regards to weapons. In these areas, it would not necessarily be unusual to see a young man with a weapon, as he is probably going hunting or to the shooting range. After all, these are also primarily rural or suburban areas. They tend to be communities that were relatively affluent, particularly where the fatality count was high. While most incidents involved fewer than six fatalities, an upward trajectory has been driven by a few high fatality incidents. Rather than an aberration, these high-fatality incidents seem to be increasing in number. Every school-based mass shooting in 2018 occurred in the South. Should the South become the new epicenter of school-based mass shootings, it would be consistent with the fact that overall the South had the most supportive regional gun culture.

There were differences in the type of shooter for the different school levels that have implications for response strategies. Every elementary school mass shooter was external to the school. Elementary schools however sustained a disproportionate number of fatalities in relation to their number of incidents. Since there is no way to know who is going to come in, schools rely on making it difficult to get into the school. In contrast, the shooter in every high school mass shooting was a high school student who could easily gain access. While high schools also hardened their exteriors as well as interiors, the student status of a potential school shooter means that the possibility exists that the appropriate support services in schools can reduce the likelihood that these incidents will occur.

In looking at perpetrators, it is important to shift the focus from perceiving shooters as mentally ill to recognizing that social and environmental factors can contribute to poor mental health (i.e., stress, anxiety) or emotional distress. These are not mental illnesses. A very small minority may suffer from severe mental illnesses, but that is the exception rather than the norm. The continued association of mass shootings with the thought that the perpetrator must be mentally ill enables avoidance of the fact that school shooters do not look like how criminals are expected to look. Therefore, there has to be an explanation for their behavior. Until it is accepted that most school shooters are white males, in relatively affluent suburban and rural communities, it will be impossible to direct intervention and prevention efforts in the right direction. The missed opportunities for intervention will continue. A twofold approach is needed: remove guns from the hands of children and increase support services in schools to address the needs of all students.

Accomplishing these actions means it is necessary to uncouple ourselves from existing federal firearms policies. If individuals with common sense and goodwill on both sides of the issue were going to attempt to find that common ground spoken of by Metzl et al., where would it be, and what would it look like? The first step to be taken is a simple but monumental one. It only requires the recognition that effective change has to happen on the federal level. Until it does, the patchwork mosaic of federal, state, and local laws that represents U.S. gun policy will continue to allow weapons to slip across porous state borders into a restrictive state from a less restrictive neighboring state.

A federal minimum age of twenty-one years for long gun ownership or possession is an example of the type of action which should be considered. It is acknowledged that while possession of both alcohol and cigarettes is prohibited for those under the age of twenty-one, it is not uncommon for minors to gain access. The prohibition is about laying the groundwork for a gradual rather than an immediate change in behavior. One argument for raising the drinking age was that eighteen-year-old high school students were able to legally buy alcohol, which they then shared with their underage friends. Raising the drinking age to twenty-one was, therefore, also about moving alcohol access out of high schools. A federal minimum age for long gun possession is about making it less common to see young adolescents walking around with guns. As a concession to those already legally able to possess long guns, they could be *grandfathered in*, with the minimum age raised incrementally.

An important step would be to limit magazine size. This limitation would, at a minimum, require shooters to insert a new clip and would interrupt the spray of ammunition. It might give children and teachers a few seconds to run to another room and hide. This limitation would not interfere with the ability to own these types of weapons. These steps have the potential to minimize the frequency and impact of school-based mass shootings. It is time to return to a federal firearm framework that regulates firearms and not just individuals.

The key to finding common ground in the search for solutions to mass shootings asserted by Metzl et al. is to recognize what they identified as a complex intertwining between mental illness, gun access issues, gun crime issues, and social networks. For instance, they suggested that mass shootings reflected group psychologies in addition to individual psychologies.[2] The group psychology, they asserted, was based on social issues such as displaced male anxiety about demographic change and the impact of being surrounded by and needing so many guns.[3] Notions of displaced male anxiety are often tied up with nuances of gendered and racialized expectations. These expectations translate into who or what is considered dangerous. Until that cycle can be broken, it produces an endless feedback loop that will continue to overlook those who typically perpetuate school-based mass shootings.

There are two important questions to be considered. First, why are firearms the one dangerous product where federal law protects manufacturers from being sued?[4] For that matter, why are firearms owners protected from suit if their gun kills someone?[5] If a child enters a yard and drowns in the homeowner's swimming pool, that homeowner will most likely be sued. A swimming pool is an "attractive nuisance" which attracts others, particularly children. Therefore, the owner is legally required to take extra steps to ensure that despite being attracted, children are unable to enter. The question is whether putting a child safety lock on a gun should be sufficient to absolve an owner of liability when that gun is used, particularly by a minor child who lives in their house? It is acknowledged that some will be disturbed at the thought that perhaps parents could be sued if their child takes the parents' weapon, walks into their school, and proceeds to slaughter every student, teacher, and administrator they encounter. But why is that any more disturbing than the thought of a dangerous instrumentality being available to a child in the first place who can then use it to do harm to others?

Even before you get to the 2nd Amendment in the U.S. Constitution there is the preamble to the Constitution. "We the people of the United States, in order to form a more perfect union, establish justice, insure domestic tranquility, provide for the common defense, promote the general welfare, and secure the blessings of liberty to ourselves and our posterity, do ordain and establish this Constitution for the United States of America. " This preamble is generally conceded as defining the common good.[6] It is a common good that rests on rights that may be in conflict and, therefore, will often need balancing. Even if the 2nd Amendment to the U.S. Constitution does mean that anyone can own any weapons they want, in any quantity, considerations of the common good, as distinct from the individual desire, requires a reconsideration of the current national stance on gun policy if we want a nation where children can go to school safely and without fear.

NOTES

1. (Vizzard 2015).
2. (Metzl and MacLeish 2015).
3. (Metzl and MacLeish 2015).
4. *See*, The Protection of Lawful Commerce in Arms Act 2005.
5. *See*, The Child Safety Lock Act of 2005.
6. (Galston 2013).

References

1789. "United States Constitution."

2018. March 9. https://massshootingtracker.org/.

Agnich, Laura E. 2015. "A Comparative Analysis of Attempted and Completed School-Based Mass Murder Attacks." *American Journal of Criminal Justice* 1–22.

Altimari, Dave. 2019. "State Supreme Court Overturns Lower Court Ruling, Says Sandy Hook Families Can Sue Gun Manufacturer Remington." *Hartford Current.* March 14. Accessed August 10, 2019. https://www.courant.com/news/connecticut/hc-news-sandy-hook-gun-ruling-20190314-pwcw3qncazb7zkitbbkocmplka-story.html.

Anderson, Curt. 2019. "Parkland School Shooting Trial Delayed at Least Until Summer." *APNews.com.* December 19. Accessed December 20, 2019. https://apnews.com/1037de446ee85e2199ec670e6e3e60bc.

Anonymous, Interview by Angelyn Spaulding Flowers. 2019. "Arming Teachers." June 5.

Aseltine Jr, Robert, Susan Gore, and Jennifer Gordon. 2000. "Life Stress, Anger and Anxiety, and Delinquency: An Empirical Test of General Strain Theory." *Journal of Health and Social Behavior* 41(3), 256–275.

Associated Press. 2017. "Tax Day 2017: Which State Sends the Most Federal Taxes to D.C.?" *Fortune.* April 16. Accessed September 12, 2019. https://fortune.com/2017/04/16/tax-day-2017-most-tax-dollars/.

Baker, Jennifer Edwards. 2019. "Dayton GOP Congressman Whose Daughter Was Across Street from Mass Shooting Backs Ban on 'Military-Style' Guns, Magazine Limits." *MySunCoast.* August 7. Accessed September 4, 2019. https://www.mysuncoast.com/2019/08/07/dayton-gop-congressman-whose-daughter-was-across-street-mass-shooting-backs-ban-military-style-guns-magazine-limits/.

Beretta.com. n.d. "Px4 Storm Full." Accessed June 20, 2019. http://www.beretta.com/en-us/px4-storm-full/.

Biery Golick, Keith. 2017. "The Untold Story Behind Madison's School Shooting." *Cinncinati.com.* February 28. Accessed August 12, 2019. https://www.cincinna

ti.com/story/news/2017/02/28/how-school-shooting-victim-learned-forgive/888
28724/.

Blum, Dinur, and Christian Gonzalez Jaworski. 2016. "From Suicide and Strain to
Mass Murder." *Social Science and Public Policy* 53(4), 408–413.

Brady Campaign to Prevent Gun Violence. 2015. "The Brady Campaign State
Scorecard." *Washington*. March.

Brown, Joshua D, and Amie J Goodin. 2018. "Mass Casualty Shooting Venues,
Types of Firearms, and Age of Perpetrators in the United States 1982–2018."
American Journal of Public Health, October: 108(10), 1385–1387.

Bureau of Alcohol, Tobacco, and Firearms. 2019. "Number of Registered Firearms in
the United States in 2019 by State." *Firearms Commerce in the United States 2019*.
August. Accessed November 2, 2019. https://www.statista.com/statistics/215655/
number-of-registered-weapons-in-the-us-by-state/.

Bushmaster Firearms. 2006. *Bushmaker Operating and Safety Instruction Manual*.
Madison: Bushmaster Firearms.

CBS News AP. 2017. "Freeman High School Shooting: Suspect Says He Was Bullied
Police Documents Say." *CBS News*. September 14. Accessed August 1, 2019. https
://www.cbsnews.com/news/freeman-high-school-shooting-suspect-said-he-was-bu
llied-police-documents-say/.

Center for Disease Control, National Center for Health Statistics. 2019. "Firearm
Mortality by State." January 10. Accessed November 12, 2019. https://www.cdc
.gov/nchs/pressroom/sosmap/firearm_mortality/firearm.htm.

Chan, Melissa. 2019. "Supreme Court Says Sandy Hook Families Can Sue the
Remington Gun Maker." *Time*. November 12. Accessed November 15, 2019. https
://time.com/5725068/sandy-hook-remington-supreme-court/.

City of Parkland. n.d. "Parkland Florida." *Parkland Florida Official Website*.
Accessed October 21, 2019. https://www.cityofparkland.org/.

Clark, Jessica. 2014. "Cokeville Elementary School Bombing." *WyoHistory.org: A Project
of the Wyoming State Historical Society*. November 8, 2014. Accessed August 6, 2019.
https://www.wyohistory.org/encyclopedia/cokeville-elementary-school-bombing.

CNN Library (a). 2019. "Sandy Hook School Shootings Fast Facts." *CNN*. March
27. Accessed June 3, 2019. https://www.cnn.com/2013/06/07/us/connecticut-shoo
tings-fast-facts/index.html.

———— (b). 2019. "Virginia Tech Shootings Fast Facts." *CNN*. April 4. Accessed
August 6, 2019. https://www.cnn.com/2013/10/31/us/virginia-tech-shootings-fast
-facts/index.html.

Colt. n.d. "Colt AR-15 Semi-Auto 9MM." Accessed July 7, 2019. https://www.col
t.com/api.php?action=specsheet&product_id=24197&title=Colt%20AR-15%20S
emi- Auto%209mm.

Cook, Phillip J, and Harold A Pollack. 2017. "Reducing Access to Guns by Violent
Offenders." *RSF: The Russell Sage Foundation Journal of the Social Science* 1–36.

Cullen, Dave. 2009. *Columbine*. New York: Hachette Book Group.

————. 2019. *Parkland*. New York: Harper.

D'Angelo, Bob, and Cox Media Group National Content Desk. 2018. "Accused
Santa Fe Shooter Won't Get Death Penalty – And Could Get Paroled Someday."

Atlanta Journal Constitution. May 20. https://www.ajc.com/news/accused-santa-shooter-won-get-death-penalty-and-could-get-paroled-someday/s8Mwcf2D6xBaV8ldvZbSZJ/.

Danner, Chas. 2019. "Everything We Know About the El Paso Walmart Massacre." *Intelligencer*. August 7. Accessed September 4, 2019. http://nymag.com/intelligencer/2019/08/everything-we-know-about-the-el-paso-walmart-shooting.html.

de la Garza, Alejandro, and Michael Zenee. 2019. "Dayton Shooting Lasted Just 32 Seconds and Left 9 Dead." *Time*. August 9. Accessed September 4, 2019. https://time.com/5643405/what-to-know-shooting-dayton-ohio/.

de Vogue, Ariane, and Sarah Jorgenson. 2019. "Remington Arms Company Asks Supreme Court to Take Up Case Related to Sandy Hook Shooting." *CNN Politics*. August 1. Accessed August 10, 2019. https://www.cnn.com/2019/08/01/politics/sandy-hook-remington-arms-supreme-court/index.html.

Dickey, Fred. 2013. "Column: Killer Recounts Santana High shooting." *The San Diego Union-Tribune*. May 10. Accessed September 1, 2019. https://www.sandiegouniontribune.com/news/columnists/sdut-charles-andy-williams-santana-high-school-shooting-2013may10-htmlstory.html.

District of Columbia et al. v. Heller. 2008. 554 U.S. 570; 28 S. Ct. 2783; 171 L. Ed. 2d 637.

Duva, Nicholas. 2014. "Gun Laws Vary by State - CNBC Explains." *CNBC*. November 20. Accessed June 28, 2019. https://www.cnbc.com/2014/11/20/gun-laws-vary-state-by-state-cnbc-explains.html.

Eldridge, Ellen. 2016. "Heritage High School Shooter Gets Early Parole." *The Atlanta Journal-Constitution*. July 15. Accessed August 6, 2019. https://www.ajc.com/news/crime--law/heritage-high-school-shooter-gets-early-parole/rTieNcNKltpdmRtxUugIGJ/.

Enger, John. 2015. "The Shooting at Red Lake: What happened?" *MPR News*. March 28. Accessed June 3, 2019. https://www.mprnews.org/story/2015/03/18/red-lake-shooting-explained.

Farr, Kathryn. 2018. "Adolescent Rampage School Shootings: Responses to Failing Masculinity Performances by Already Troubled Boys." *Gender Issues* 73–97.

Fast, Jonathan. 2008. *Ceremonial Violence: Understanding Columbine and Other Rampage Shootings*. New York: Overlook Press.

Federal Bureau of Investigation, Behavioral Analysis Unit, National Center for the Analysis of Violent Crime. 2005. *Serial Murder: Multi-Disciplinary Perspectives for Investigators*. Washington: FBI.

Fein, Albert. 2002. *There and Back Again: School Shootings As Experienced by School Leaders*. Lanham: Rowman and Littlefield Education.

Felson, Richard, and Paul-Phillippe Pare. 2010. "Gun Culture or Honor Culture? Explaining Regional and Race Differences in Gun Weapons Carrying." *Social Forces* 88(3), 1358–1380.

Fox, Ben. 2001. "Teen Who Admitted to School Shooting Commits Suicide While in Jail." *The Berkeley Daily Planet*. October 30. Accessed August 6, 2019. http://www.berkeleydailyplanet.com/issue/2001-10-30/article/7909.

Fox, Cybelle, and David Harding. 2005. "School Shootings As Organized Deviance." *Sociology of Education* 78(1), 69–97.

Frosh, Dan, Erin Ailworth, and Nour Malas. 2018. "Texas Shooter Spared People He Liked Court Document Says." *Wall Street Journal*. May 19. https://www .wsj.com/articles/texas-shooter-spared-students-he-liked-court-document-says-15 26735627.

Galston, William Arthur. 2013. "The Common Good: Theoretical Content, Practical Utility." *Daedalus* 142(2), 9–14.

Giffords Law Center to Prevent Gun Violence. 2018. "Assault Weapons State by State." Accessed July 29, 2019. https://lawcenter.giffords.org/gun-laws/state-law/ 50-state-summaries/assault-weapons-state-by-state/.

——— (a). n.d. "Categories of Prohibited People." Accessed July 12, 2019. https ://lawcenter.giffords.org/gun-laws/policy-areas/who-can-have-a-gun/categories-of -prohibited-people/.

——— (b). n.d. "Universal Background Checks." Accessed July 28, 2019. https:/ /lawcenter.giffords.org/gun-laws/policy-areas/background-checks/universal-back ground-checks/.

GlockStore.com. n.d. "Glock 23-.40S&W." Accessed June 25, 2019. https://www.glo ckstore.com/Glock-23-40S-W.

Government Accounting Office. 2018. *K-12 Education: Discipline Disparities for Black Students, Boys, and Students with Disabilities*. Report to Congress. Washington: Government Accounting Office.

Gramlich, John. 2019. "What the Data Says About Gun Deaths in the U.S." *Gun Deaths in the U.S.: 10 Key Questions Answered*. August 16. Accessed November 12, 2019. https://www.pewresearch.org/fact-tank/2019/08/16/what-the-data-says -about-gun-deaths-in-the-u-s/.

Gumbel, Andrew. 2009. "The Truth About Columbine." *The Guardian*. April 16. Accessed October 1, 2019. https://www.theguardian.com/world/2009/apr/17/colu mbine-massacre-gun-crime-us.

———. n.d. "Guns in the United States Firearms, Gun Law and Gun Control." Accessed March 21, 2017. http://www.gunpolicy.org/firearms/region/united-states.

Hagman, Maureen. 2016. "4 Hurt, 14-Year-Old Student Charged in Madison Jr/Sr High School Shooting." *WLWT5*. March 1. Accessed August 12, 2019. https:// www.wlwt.com/article/4-hurt-14-year-old-student-charged-in-madison-jr-sr-high -school-shooting/3562876#.

Hamasaki, Sonya, and Darran Simon. 2017. "Student One of 3 Dead in San Bernardino Shooting." *CNN.com*. April 11. Accessed June 11, 2019. https://www .cnn.com/2017/04/10/us/san-bernardino-school-shooting/index.html.

Hanna, Jason, Dakin Andone, Keith Allen, and Steve Almasy. 2018. "Alleged Shooter at Texas High School Spared People He Liked, Court Document Says." *CNN*. May 19. Accessed October 23, 2019. https://www.cnn.com/2018/05/18/us/t exas-school-shooting/index.html.

Hanna, Jason, and Holly Yan. 2017. "Sutherland Springs Church Shooting: What We Know." *CNN*. November 7. Accessed June 12, 2019. https://www.cnn.com/2017/ 11/05/us/texas-church-shooting-what-we-know/index.html.

Harvard School of Public Health. 2008. "Gun Prevalence and Suicide Rank by State." *News Magazine*. Spring. Accessed October 5, 2019. https://www.hsph.harvard.edu /news/magazine/spr08gunprevalence/.

Hi-Point Firearms. n.d. "Model 995." Accessed July 6, 2019. https://www.hi-point firearms.com/hi-point-carbines/hi-point-9mm-carbine.php.

History.com. 2019. "Columbine Shootings." *This Day in History*. May 8. Accessed August 4, 2019. https://www.history.com/topics/1990s/columbine-high-school-s hootings.

History.Com Editors. 2009. "Columbine Shooting." *History.com*. November 9. Accessed September 4, 2019. https://www.history.com/topics/1990s/columbine -high-school-shootings.

Hoofnagle, Mark, Elinore J Kaufman, William Schwab, and Patrick Reilly. 2019. "States with Strict Gun Laws See More Homicides When They Border States with Lax Ones." *ScienceDaily*. March 6. Accessed November 11, 2019. www.scienc edaiy.com/releases/2019/03/190306110629.htm.

Intratec Firearms. n.d. "Manual TEC-DC 9." Accessed July 6, 2019. http://pdf.text files.com/manuals/FIREARMS/intratec_tec_dc9.pdf.

Ioannou, Maria, Laura Hammond, and Olivia Simpson. 2015. "A Model for Differentiating School Shooters." *Journal of Criminal Psychology* 5(3), 188–200.

Jehan, Faisal, Viraj Pandita, Terrence O'Keeffea, Asad Azima, Arpana Jaina, Saad Taia, and Andrew Tanga. 2018. "The Burden of Firearm Violence in the United States: Stricter Laws Result in Safer States." *Journal of Injury and Violence Research*, January: 10(1), 11–16.

Karson, Michael. 2013. "Paranoia and Violence." *Psychology Today*. December 15.

Kennedy, Kelli. 2018. "Florida Shooting Suspect Was Adopted and Both of His Adoptive Parents Had Recently Died." *Business Insider*. February 15. Accessed August 20, 2019. https://www.businessinsider.com/florida-shooting-suspect-nic olas-cruz-troubled-family-life-disturbed-2018-2.

King, Kate K. 2014. "Violence in the School Setting: A School Nurse Perspective." *Online Journal of Issues in Nursing*, 19(1), 4-4.

Knopov, Anita, Rebecca Sherman, Julia Raifman, Elysia Larson, and Michael Siegel. 2019. "Household Gun Ownership and Youth Suicide Rates at the State Level, 2005–2015." *American Journal of Preventive Medicine*, 56(3), 335–342.

Kocieniewski, David, and Gary Gately. 2006. "Man Shoots 11, Killing 5 Girls, in Amish School." *The New York Times*. October 3. Accessed October 10, 2019. https://www.nytimes.com/2006/10/03/us/03amish.html%20https://www.fbi.gov/fil e-repository/active-shooter-incidents-2000-2017.pdf.

Krause, William J. 2012. *Gun Control Legislation*. Congressional Research Digital Collection. Washington: U.S. Congressional Research Service.

Krouse, William J, and Daniel J Richardson. 2015. *Mass Murder with Firearms: Incidents and Victims, 1999–2013*. Washington: Congressional Research Service.

Kutner, Max. 2015. "What Led Jaylen Fryberg to Commit the Deadliest High School Shooting in a Decade." *Newsweek*. September 16. Accessed August 10, 2019. https ://www.newsweek.com/2015/09/25/jaylen-ray-fryberg-marysville-pilchuck-high-school-shooting-372669.html.

LancasterPa.com. n.d. "Amish School Shooting." *LancasterPa.Com*. Accessed July 2, 2019. https://lancasterpa.com/amish/amish-school-shooting/.

Lane, Cotina, and Angelyn Flowers. 2019. "School-Based Mass Shooting Database."

Langman, Peter. 2010. *Why Kids Kill: Inside the Mind of School Shooters*. New York: St. Martin's Griffin.

———— (a). 2016. "School Shooters: The Myth of the Stable Home ver. 1.15." *SchoolShooters.info*. May 24. Accessed September 1, 2019. https://schoolshooters .info/school-shooters-myth-stable-home.

———— (b). 2016. "The Origins of Firearms Used in School Shootings in the United States ver. 1.1." *SchoolShooters.info*. February 4. Accessed September 1, 2019. https://schoolshooters.info/origins-firearms-used-school-shootings-united-states.

———— (a). 2017. "Education: Failures and Family Involvement ver. 1.10." *SchoolShooters.info*. April 21. Accessed September 10, 2019. https://schoolshoote rs.info/education-failures-and-family-involvement.

———— (b). 2017. *School Shooters: Understanding High School, College and Adult Perpetrators*. Lanham: Rowan and Littlefield.

———— (a). 2018. "Legal Histories of School Shooters ver. 1.3." *SchoolShooters.info* . April 25. Accessed October 10, 2019. https://schoolshooters.info/legal-histories -school-shooters.

———— (b). 2018. "School Shooters: A Miscellany ver. 1.35." *SchoolShooters.info*. December 30. Accessed August 10, 2019. https://schoolshooters.info/school-shoot ers-miscellany.

LeBrun, Marcel. 2008. *Books, Blackboards, and Bullets: School Shootings and Violence in America*. Lanham: Rowman & Littlefield Education.

Lemieux, Frederic. 2014. "Effect of Gun Culture and Firearms Laws on Gun Violence and Mass Shootings in the United States: A Multi-Level Quantitative Analysis." *International Journal of Criminal Justice Sciences* 9, 74–93.

Lenhardt, Ann Marie C, Melissa L Farrell, and Lemuel Graham. 2010. "Providing Anchors—Reclaiming Our Troubled Youth: Lessons for Leaders from a Study of 15 Targeted School Shooters." *The Educational Forum* (82)1, 104–116.

Levenson, Eric, and Joe Sterling. 2018. "These Are the Victims of the Florida School Shooting." *CNN*. February 21. Accessed August 2, 2019. https://www.cnn.com/ 2018/02/15/us/florida-shooting-victims-school/index.html.

Lofquist, Daphne, Terry Lugaila, Martin O'Connell, and Sarah Feliz. 2012. *Households and Families 2010*. 2010 Census Briefs. Washington: U.S. Census Bureau.

Logan, Joshua. 2016. "The 1998 Thurston High School Attack." *Officer.com*. July 5. https://www.officer.com/tactical/article/12228005/the-1998-thurston-high-school- attack

Lombardo, Clare, and Cory Turner. 2018. "Disparities Persist in School Discipline Says Government Watchdog." *NPR: Heard on All Things Considered*. April 4. https://www.npr.org/sections/ed/2018/04/04/590887226/persistent-disparities-in-s chool-discipline-says-government-watchdog.

Lozano, Juan A (a). 2019. "Accused Texas School Shooter Found Incompetent to Stand Trial by Three Experts, Lawyer Says." *USAToday.com*. November 4.

Accessed November 6, 2019. https://www.usatoday.com/story/news/nation/2019 /11/04/dimitrios-pagourtzis-texas-high-schooler-shooter-found-incompetent/4158 999002/.

——— (b). 2019. "Accused Texas Teen Found Incompetent to Stand Trial by Three Experts, Lawyer Says." *USA Today*. November 4. https://www.usatoday.com/story /news/nation/2019/11/04/dimitrios-pagourtzis-texas-high-schooler-shooter-found -incompetent/4158999002/.

Luca, Michael, Depak Malhotra, and Christopher Poliquin. 2019. *The Impact of Mass Shootings on Gun Policy*. Working Paper. Boston: Harvard Business School.

Lupica, Mike. 2013. "Morbid Find Suggests Murder-Obsessed Gunman Adam Lanza Plotted Newtown, Conn.'s Sandy Hook Massacre for Years." *New York Daily News*. March 25. Accessed September 20, 2019. https://www.nydailynews.com/ news/national/lupica-lanza-plotted-massacre-years-article-1.1291408?print%20h ttps://www.fbi.gov/file-repository/active-shooter-incidents-2000-2017.pdf.

Luzzader, Dan. 1999. "Loophole Protects Columbine 'Witness'." *Rocky Mountain News*. October 3. Accessed September 4, 2019. https://web.archive.org/web/20 010221030107/http://denver.rockymountainnews.com/shooting/1003robyn.shtml.

Lysiak, Matthew. 2013. *Newtown: An American Tragedy*. New York: Gallery Books.

Maag, Chris, and Ian Urbina. 2007. "Student 14, Shoots 4 and Kills Himself in Cleveland School." *The New York Times*. October 11. Accessed July 20, 2019. https://www.nytimes.com/2007/10/11/us/11cleveland.html.

———. n.d. "Mass Shooting Tracker." *Guns Are Cool Subreddit*. https://www .massshootingtracker.org/.

Margaritoff, Marco. 2019. "The Full Story Behind Columbine High School Shooters Eric Harris And Dylan Klebold." *ATI: History, Science, News*. March 8. Accessed June 12, 2019. https://allthatsinteresting.com/eric-harris-dylan-klebold-columbine-shooters.

McCluskey, Michael. 2016. *News Framing of School Shootings*. Lanham: Lexington Books.

McDonald et al. v City of Chicago, Illinois et al. 2010. 61 U.S. 742; 130 S. Ct. 3020; 177 L. Ed. 2d 894.

McGinty, Emma E, Daniel W Webster, Marian Jarlenski, and Colleen L Barry. 2014. "News Media Framing of Serious Mental Illness and Gun Violence in the United States 1997–2012." *American Journal of Public Health*, March: 104, 406–413.

Meindl, James N, and Jonathan W Ivy. 2017. "Mass Shootings: The Role of the Media in Promoting Generalized Imitation." *American Journal of Public Health,* 107, 368–370.

Metzl, Jonathan, and Kenneth MacLeish. 2015. "Mass Shootings, Mental Illness, and the Politics of American Firearms." *American Journal of Public Health* 105, 240–249.

Miller, Matthew, Lisa Hepburn, and Deborah Azrael. 2017. "Firearm Acquisition Without Background Check: Results of a National Survey." *Annals of Internal Medicine,* 166(4), 233–239.

Mingus, W, and B Zopf. 2010. "White Means Never Having to Say You're Sorry: The Racial Project in Explaining Mass Shootings." *Social Thought and Research* 31, 57–77.

Minshew, Lana M. 2018. "From the Editorial Board: On Arming K - 12 Teachers." *The High School Journal,* 101(3), 129–133.

Muschert, Glen, and Joanna Sumiala. 2012. *School Shootings: Mediatized Violence in a Global Age.* V.7. Bingley, UK: Emerald.

Nedzel, Nadia E. 2014. "Concealed Carry: The Only Way to Discourage Mass School Shootings." *Academic Questions: A Publication of the National Association of Scholars,* 27(4), 429–435.

Netstate.com. 2016. "The Geography of Colorado." *Colorado.* February 25. Accessed October 5, 2019. https://www.netstate.com/states/geography/co_geography.htm.

———. 2017. "50 State Rankings for Size." *Netstate.com.* September 9. Accessed August 11, 2019. https://www.netstate.com/states/tables/st_size.htm.

New York State Rifle and Pistol Association et al. v. City of New York, NY. 2019. Docket No. 18-280 cert. granted, 2019 WL 271961 (2019); previous 883 F.3d 45 (2d Cir. 2018) (United States Supreme Court).

New York State Rifle and Pistol Association et al. v. City of New York, NY. 2020. 590 U.S. ___.

Newman, Katherine S, Cybelle Fox, David J Harding, Jal Mehta, and Wendy Roth. 2008. Rampage: *The Social Roots of School Shootings.* New York: Basic Books.

Nickelsburg, Monica, and Amy Moreno. 2018. "Seattle Company Offers Free Facial Recognition to Schools." *GeekWire.* July 18.

Osborne, Jeffery, and Joel Capellan. 2016. "Examining Active Shooter Events Through the Rational Choice Perspective and Crime Script Analysis." *Security Journal,* (30)3, 880–902.

O'Toole, Mary Ellen. 2000. *The School Shooter: A Threat Assessment Perspective.* Washington: Federal Bureau of Investigation, United States Department of Justice.

Pack, Lauren. 2016. "Austin Hancock Told Police His 'Home Life' Prompted Shootings." *Dayton Daily News.* June 17. Accessed August 6, 2019. https://www.daytondailynews.com/news/motive-madison-high-school-shooting-revealed/6frSgslHtefcEIrURqFroO/.

Parker, Kim, Juliana Menasce Horowitz, Igielnik Ruth, J Baxter Oliphant, and Anna Brown. 2017. "Guns and Daily Life in the U.S.: Identity, Experiences, Activities, and Involvement." *Pew Research Center.* June 22. Accessed June 22, 2019. https://www.pewsocialtrends.org/2017/06/22/guns-and-daily-life-identity-experiences-and-involvement.

Plain Dealer Staff. 2019. "Chardon High School Shooting: A Guide to What Happened and How Word Spread." *Cleveland.com.* January 12. Accessed September 2, 2019. https://www.cleveland.com/metro/2012/02/chardon_high_school_shooting_a_1.html.

Podlogar, Matthew, Anna Gai, Matthew Schneider, Christopher Hagan, and Thomas Joiner. 2018. "Advancing the Prediction and Prevention of Murder-Suicide." *Journal of Aggression, Conflict, and Peace Research,* 10(3), 223–234.

Popenker, Maxim. n.d. "Saiga 12." Accessed September 6, 2019. https://modernfirearms.net/en/shotguns/russia-shotguns/sajga-12-eng/.

Powell, Nick. 2019. "Judge Officially Declare Accused Santa Fe Shooter Incompetent to Stand Trial." *Houston Chronicle.* November 15. Accessed November 21, 2019.

https://www.houstonchronicle.com/news/houston-texas/houston/article/Judge-o
fficially-declares-accused-Santa-Fe-14839317.php.

Pressley, Sue Ann. 1999. "Six Wounded in Ga. School Shooting." *The Washington Post*, May 21: A-1. https://www.washingtonpost.com/wp-srv/national/longterm/juvmurders/stories/conyers052199.htm.

Public Broadcasting Service. 2019. "How Limiting High-Capacity Magazines Could Reduce the Carnage in Mass Shooting." *PBS News Hour*. August 22. Accessed September 4, 2019. https://www.pbs.org/newshour/show/how-limiting-high-cap acity-magazines-could-reduce-the-carnage-in-mass-shootings.

Public Law 110-180. 2007. "NICS Improvement Act."

Public Law 103-159; 107 STAT 1536. 1993. "The Brady Handgun Violence Prevention Act." November 30.

Public Law 103-322; 108 STAT 1796. 1994. "The Violent Crime Control and Law Enforcement Act." September 13.

Public Law 109-92; 119 STAT 2095; 15 U.S.C. §§ 7901-7903. 2005. "Protection of Lawful Commerce in Arms Act." October 26.

Public Law 99-308, 100 STAT. 449. 1986. "The Firearms Owners' Protection Act." May 19.

Public Law 90-618. 1968. "Gun Control Act." October 22.

Purdum, Todd S. 2001. "Shooting at School Leaves 2 Dead and 13 Hurt." *New York Times*, March 6: A-1.

RAND. 2018. "The Effects of Minimum Age Requirements." *Gun Policy in America*. March 2. Accessed May 15, 2019. https://www.rand.org/research/gun-policy/anal ysis/minimum-age.html.

Rasmussen, Cecilia. 1997. "A Principal's Bloody Rampage." *Los Angeles Times*. July 20. http://articles.latimes.com/1997/jul/20/local/me-14688.

Red Lake Nation. 2014. "Tribal Government." *Red Lake Nation*. Accessed August 15, 2019. http://www.redlakenation.org/tribal-government.

Reeping, Paul, Magdalena Cerdo, Bindu Kalesan, Douglas Wiebe, Sandro Galea, and Charles Branas. 2019. "State Gun Laws, Gun Ownership, and Mass Shootings in the US: Cross-Sectional Time Series." *The BMJ*. March 6. Accessed June 20, 2019. https://www.bmj.com/content/364/bmj.l542.

Rice, Timothy, and Leon Hoffman. 2015. "Adolescent Mass Shootings: Developmental Considerations in Light of Sandy Hook." *International Journal of Adolescent Medical Health,* 27(2), 183–187.

Riley, Jason. 2019. "Lawsuit: Marshall County School Shooter Obsessed with Guns, Nazi Regime." *WDRB.News*. January 24. Accessed September 4, 2019. https://ww w.wdrb.com/in-depth/lawsuit-marshall-county-school-shooter-obsessed-with-guns -nazi-regime/article_60596d60-1fff-11e9-a2a3-0bccb6ab83d8.html.

Ruger (a). n.d. "Instruction Manual for Ruger Mark II." Accessed July 6, 2019. www .ruger.com.

——— (b). n.d. "Instruction Manual for Ruger Mark III." Accessed July 3, 2019. www.ruger.com.

Ruggles, Kelly V, and Sonali Rajan. 2014. "Gun Possession Among American Youth: A Discovery-Based Approach to Understand Gun Violence." *PLoS One,*

9(11), *111893*. Accessed July 12, 2019. https://journals.plos.org/plosone/article?id=10.1371/journal.pone.0111893.

Sanchez, Roy, and Ed Payne. 2016. "Charleston Church Shooting: Who Is Dylann Roof?" *CNN*. December 16. Accessed September 4, 2019. https://www.cnn.com/2015/06/19/us/charleston-church-shooting-suspect/index.html.

Sayers, Justice, and Andrew Wolfson. 2018. "Police: Teen Saw School Shooting As Experiment." *Courier Journal*. March 8. Accessed September 15, 2019. https://www.courier-journal.com/story/news/local/2018/03/07/marshall-county-school-shooting-gabe-parker-experiment-motive/403035002/.

Seigel, Michael, and Emily Rothman. 2016. "Firearm Ownership and the Murder of Women in the United States: Evidence That the State-Level Firearm Ownership Rate Is Associated with the Nonstranger Femicide Rate." *Violence and Gender,* 3(1), 20–26.

Siegel, M, M Pahn, Z Xuan, E Fleegler, and D Hemenway. 2019. "The Impact of State Firearm Laws on Homicide and Suicide Deaths in the USA, 1991–2016: A Panel Study." *Journal of General Internal Medicine* 2021–2028.

Simon, Dan, Eric Leveson, and Darron Simon. 2019. "Assault-Style Rifle Used in Gilroy Shooting Could Not Be Sold in California, State Attorney General Says." *CNN.com*. July 29. Accessed September 4, 2019. https://www.cnn.com/2019/07/29/us/gilroy-california-food-festival-shooting-monday/index.html.

Simonite, Tom. 2019. "The Delicate Ethics of Using Facial Recognition Software in Schools." *Wired*. October 19.

Skeem, Jennifer, and Edward Mulvey. 2020. "What Role Does Serious Mental Illness Play in Mass Shootings and How Should We Address It?" *Criminology and Public Policy,* 19(1), 85–108.

Statistica. n.d. "Median Age of the U.S. Population 1968 to 2018." *Society: Demographics*. Accessed September 20, 2019. https://www.statista.com/statistics/241494/median-age-of-the-us-population/.

Sterngold, James. 2001. "Police Say Student Gunman Was Seeking School Official." *New York Times*, March 24: A-8.

The Brady Campaign to Prevent Gun Violence. 2015. *The Brady Campaign State Scorecard*. Washington: bradycampaign.org.

The New York Times. 1975. "Upstate Youth in Sniper Trial a Suicide." *The New York Times*. November 2. https://www.nytimes.com/1975/11/02/archives/upstate-youth-in-sniper-trial-a-suicide.html.

Towers, Sherry, Andres Gomez-Lievano, Maryam Khan, Anuj Mubayi, and Carlos Castillo-Chavez. 2015. "Contagion in Mass Killings and School Shootings." *PLoS One,* 10(7). J

Turkewitz, Julie, and Jesse Bidgood. 2018. "Who Is Dimitrios Pagourtzis, the Texas Shooting Suspect." *New York Times*. May 18. https://www.nytimes.com/2018/05/18/us/dimitrios-pagourtzis-gunman-texas-shooting.html.

United States v Miller et al. 1939. 307 U.S. 175.

U.S. Bureau of the Census. 2019. "Table H-8 Median Household Income by State 1984–2018." *Current Population Survey, Annual Social and Economic*

Supplements. August 29. Accessed November 16, 2019. https://www.census.gov
/data/tables/time-series/demo/income-poverty/historical-income-households.html.

U.S. Census Bureau (a). 2000. *Census 2000 Summary File 1.* Census Data set. Washington: U.S. Census Bureau.

——— (b). 2000. *Census 2000 Summary File 3.* Census Datasets. Washington: U.S. Census Bureau.

——— (a). 2010. *2010 Census Summary File 1.* Census Dataset. Washington: U.S. Census Bureau.

——— (b). 2010. *Educational Attainment: 2006–2010 American Community Survey 5-Year Estimates.* Census Dataset. Washington: U.S. Census Bureau.

———. 2012. *2008–2012 American Community Survey.* Census Dataset. Washington: U.S. Census Bureau.

———. 2017. *2013–2017 American Community Survey 5-Year Estimates.* Census Dataset. Washington: U.S. Census.

———. 2018. "1Table 1. Annual Estimates of the Resident Population for the United States, Regions, States, and Puerto Rico: April 1, 2010 to July 1, 2018." *2018 National and State Population Estimates.* December 19. Accessed September 12, 2019. https://www.census.gov/newsroom/press-kits/2018/pop-estimates-national -state.html.

——— (a). n.d. "American Community Survey Demographic and Housing Estimates 2005–2009."

——— (b). n.d. "Map of the United States Showing Census Divisions and Regions." Accessed June 22, 2019. https://www.census.gov/prod/1/gen/95statab/preface.pdf.

U.S. Census Bureau Population Division. 2013. "Annual Estimates of the Resident Population: April 1, 2010 to July 1, 2012." *American Fact Finder.* May. Accessed September 5, 2019. https://factfinder.census.gov/faces/tableservices/jsf/pages/ productview.xhtml?src=bkmk.

U.S. Fish and Wildlife Service. 2004. "Historical Hunting License Data: Hunting State License Holder Certifications—1999." *Wildlife and Sport Fish Restoration Program.* December 2. Accessed June 15, 2019. https://wsfrprograms.fws.gov/S ubpages/LicenseInfo/Hunting.htm.

———. n.d. "National Hunting License Data Calculation Year 2018." Accessed October 2, 2019. https://wsfrprograms.fws.gov/subpages/licenseinfo/Natl%20Hun ting%20License%20Report%202018.pdf.

USACarry. n.d. "Gun Ranges." *USACarry.* Accessed November 10, 2019. https://ww w.usacarry.com/directory/category/gun-ranges/.

Vizzard, William J. 2015. "The Current and Future State of Gun Policy in the United States." *The Journal of Criminal Law and Criminology,* 104(4), 881–904.

Voght, Kara. 2019. "House Democrats Are Holding the First Vote on Gun Control in More Than a Decade." *Mother Jones.* February 27. Accessed June 5, 2019. https:// www.motherjones.com/politics/2019/02/house-democrats-are-holding-the-first-vo te-on-gun-control-in-more-than-a-decade/.

Wallman, Brittany, and Megan O'Matz. 2019. "Violent Kids Take Over Florida's Classrooms and They Have the Law on Their Side." *Sun Sentinel.* December 10.

Accessed December 11, 2019. https://projects.sun-sentinel.com/teenage-time-bom
bs/how-schools-manage-violent-kids/.

Weill, Kelly, and Kate Briquelet. 2018. "Dimitrios Pagourtzis, Texas Shooting
Suspect, Posted Neo-Nazi Imagery Online." *Daily Beast.* May 18. Accessed
August 20, 2019. https://www.thedailybeast.com/dimitrios-pagourtzis-reportedly
-idd-as-santa-fe-texas-shooting-suspect.

Welch, Chris. 2011. "Slain Assistant Principal Sent Home Because of Trespass
Charge." *CNN.* January 6. Accessed November 30, 2019. http://www.cnn.com/2
011/CRIME/01/06/nebraska.school.shooting/index.html.

Welton, Evonn, Shernavaz Vakil, and Bridgie Ford. 2014. "Beyond Bullying:
Consideration of Additional Research for the Assessment and Prevention of
Potential Rampage School Violence in the United States." *Education Research
International*, 2014, 1–9.

Wilkie, Christina. 2013. "Connecticut Passes Nation's Strictest Gun Law in Wake of
Sandy Hook Massacre." *Huffpost.* April 4. Accessed May 1, 2019. https://www.huf
fpost.com/entry/connecticut-gun-control-sandy-hook-law_n_3011625.

Wilson, Conrad. 2018. "20 Years Ago, Oregon School Shooting Ended a Bloody
Season." *NPR National Public Radio.* May 22. https://www.npr.org/2018/05/22
/612465197/20-years-ago-oregon-school-shooting-ended-a-bloody-season.

Wolfson, Andrews. 2019. "A Year Later: Marshall County High School Shooting and
the Prosecution." *Louisville Courier Journal.* January 18. Accessed September 2,
2019. https://www.courier-journal.com/story/news/crime/2019/01/17/marshall-c
ounty-high-school-kentucky-shooting-a-year-later/2593728002/.

World Atlas. n.d. "The Officially Recognized Four Regions and Nine Divisions of the
United States." Accessed June 22, 2019. https://www.worldatlas.com/articles/the-
officially-recognized-four-regions-and-nine-divisions-of-the-united-states.html.

World Population Review. 2019. "World Population Review." *Omaha Nebraska.*
October 29. Accessed November 30, 2019. http://worldpopulationreview.com/us
-cities/omaha-population/.

Zewe, Charles (Contributor). 1997. "Teen Pleads Innocent in High School Shooting."
October 2. http://www.cnn.com/US/9710/02/miss.shooting.folo/.

Zimmerman, GM, and EE Fridel. 2019. "Contextualizing Homicide-Suicide:
Examining How Ecological Gun Availability Affects Homicide-Suicide at
Multiple Levels of Analysis." *Homicide Studies,* 24(2), 1–27.

Index

About the Authors

Angelyn Spaulding Flowers, J.D., PhD, is professor and coordinator of the Crime, Justice, and Security Studies Program at the University of the District of Columbia. She is the founding director of the University's graduate program in Homeland Security. A social scientist with an interest in social structures and community destabilization, she has authored chapters appearing in a diverse range of books from cybersecurity to emergency management to public policy. Included among her chapters are "Emergency Management and Vulnerable Populations" appearing in Abbott, Ernest and Hetzel, Otto (Eds) *Homeland Security and Emergency Management: A Guide for State and Local Governments*, 3rd edition (published by the American Bar Association, 2018); "The Dynamics of Poverty in the District of Columbia" in R. Walters and T. M. Travis (Eds). *Democratic Destiny and the District of Columbia: Federal Politics and Public Policy in an Administered Political System* (published by Lexington Books, 2010). She has also had articles appearing in the *Journal of Homeland Security and Emergency Management*, *Technology and Society Magazine IEEE*, and the *International Journal of Interdisciplinary Social Science*

Cotina Lane Pixley currently serves as a clinical instructor in the Crime, Justice, and Security Studies Program at the University of the District of Columbia. She holds a bachelor of arts degree in Administration of Justice from the University of the District of Columbia and a master of science degree in Homeland Security, also from the University of the District of Columbia, where her focus was emergency management. Cotina values community engagement and social action. She has a background in research, training and evaluation, service and outreach to government agencies, community-based organizations, faith-based organizations, and other nonprofit entities. Cotina served as a Sergeant in the U.S. Army and has worked on and supported research in the areas of risk communication and community resilience, ranging from the development and utilization of effective risk communications and the examination of such communications; to the examination of K–12 school-based mass shootings in the United States. Cotina is currently a PhD student in the Disaster Science and Management Program at the University of Delaware.